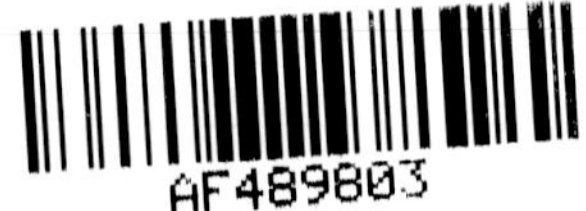

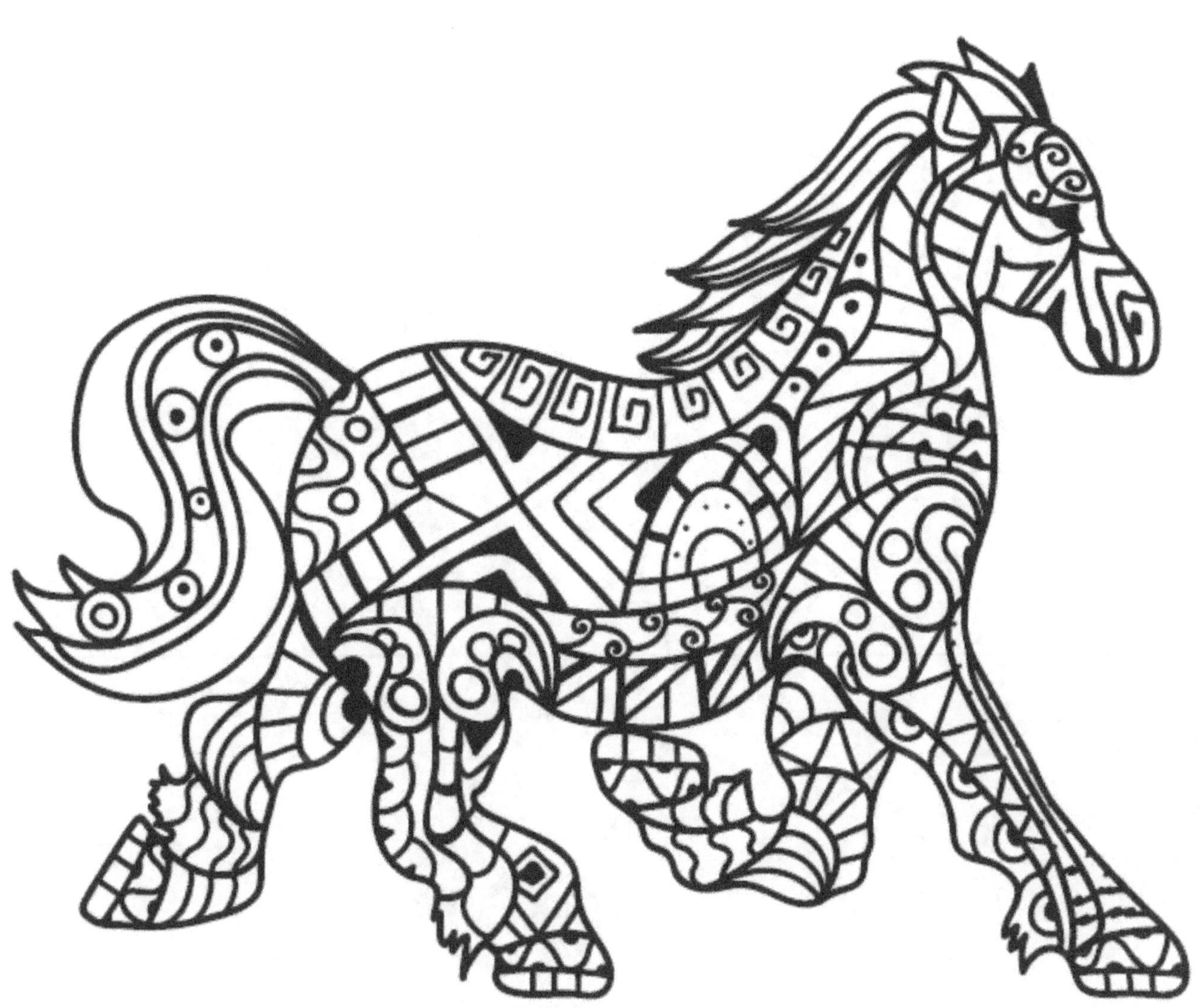

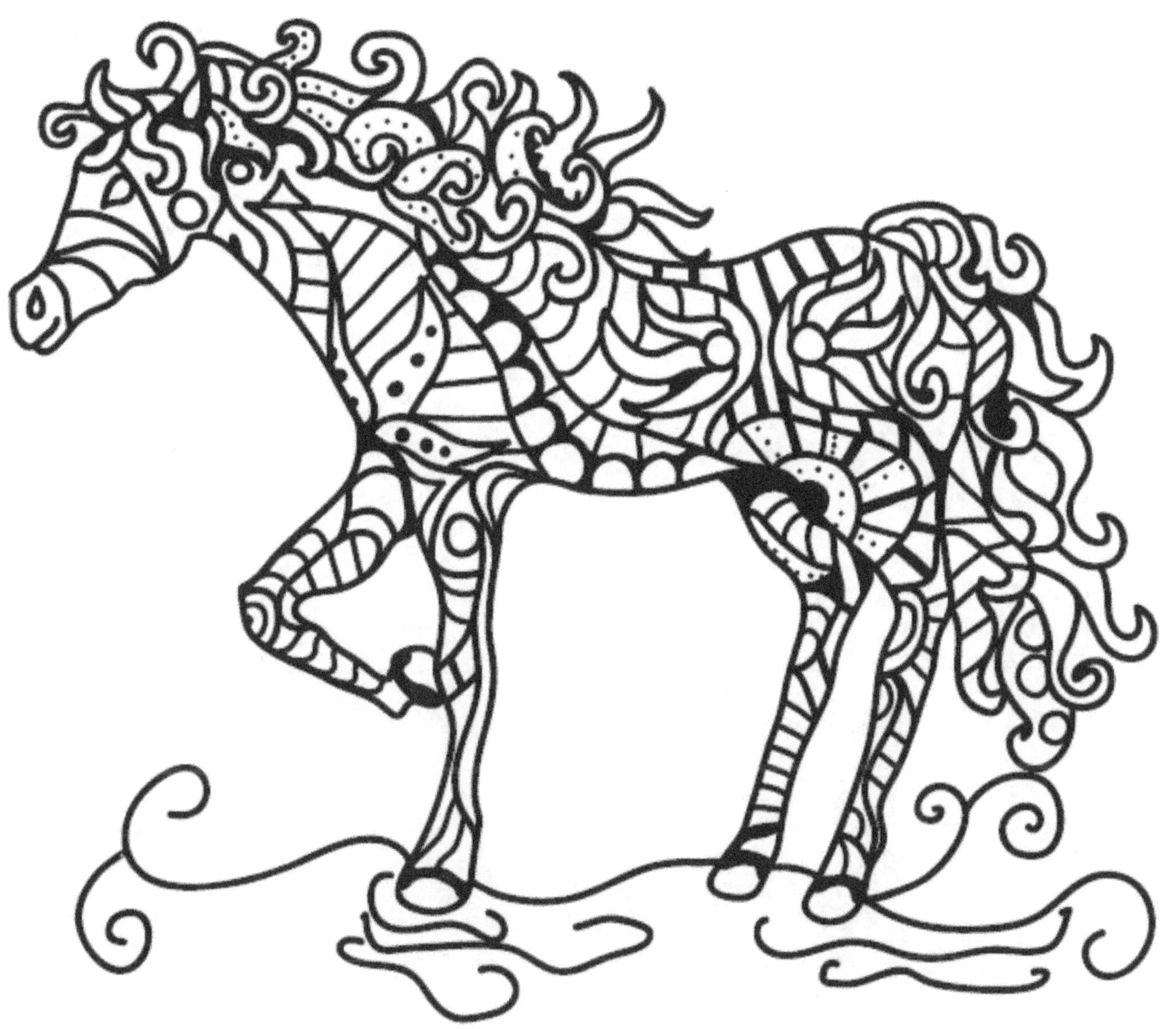

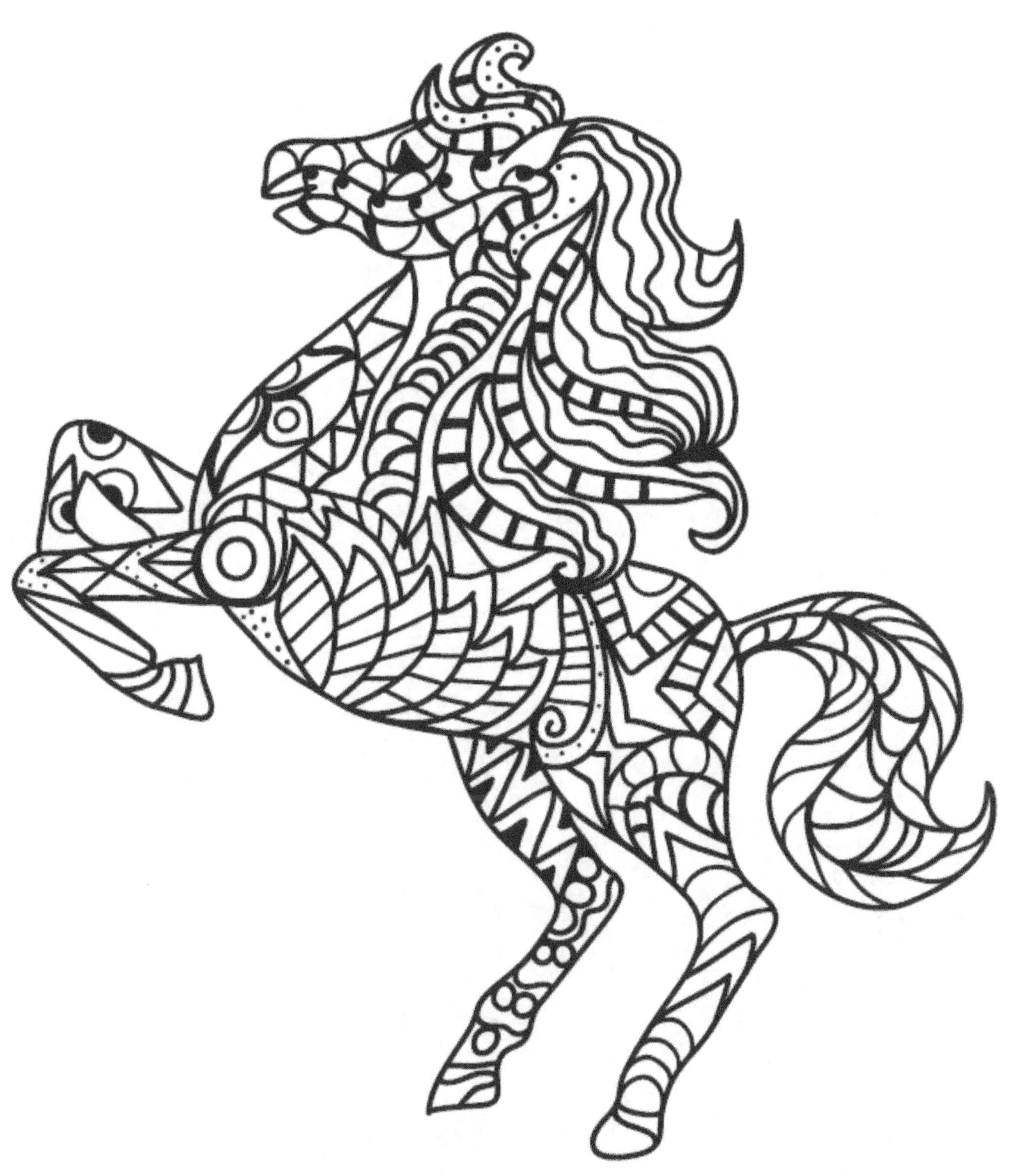

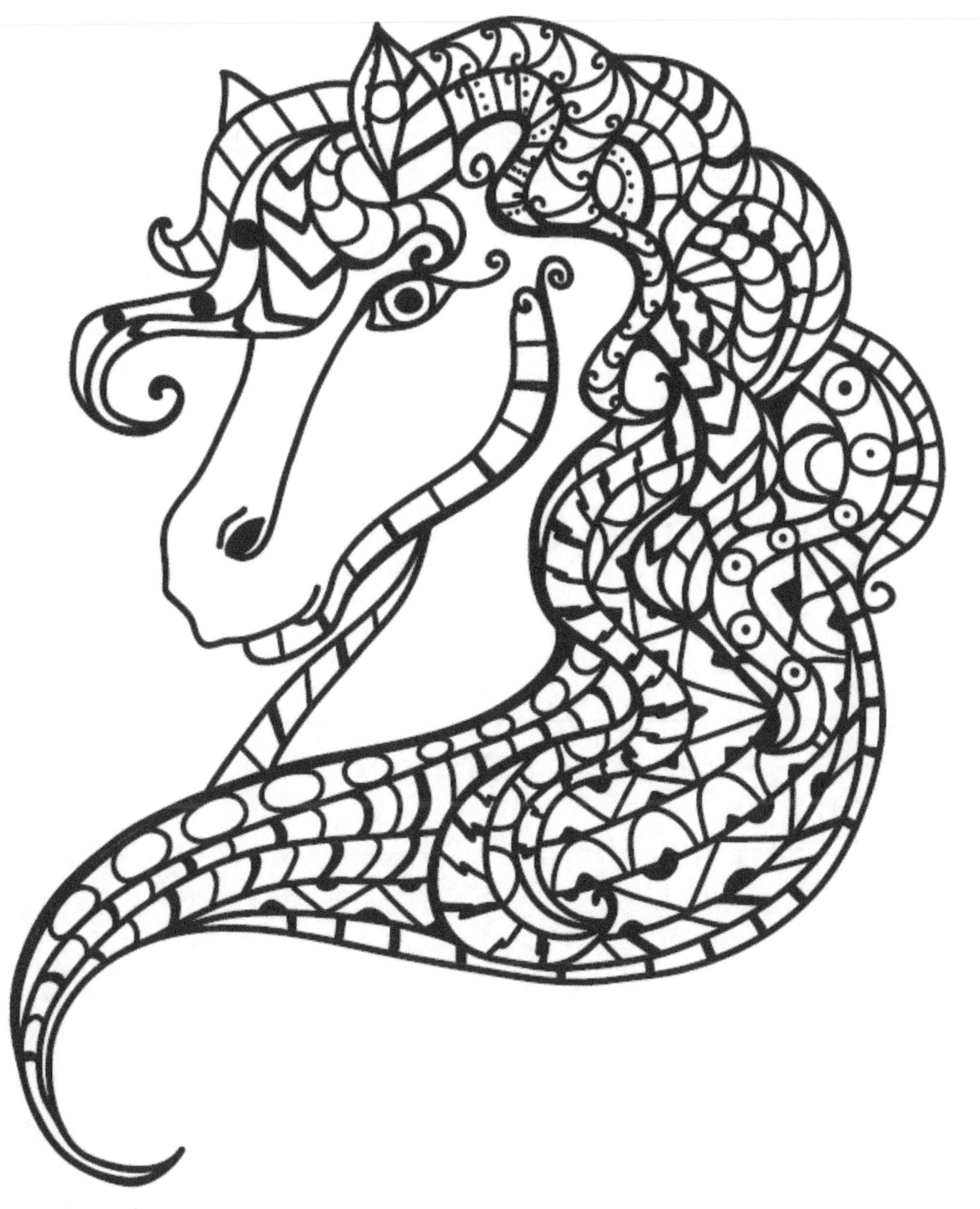

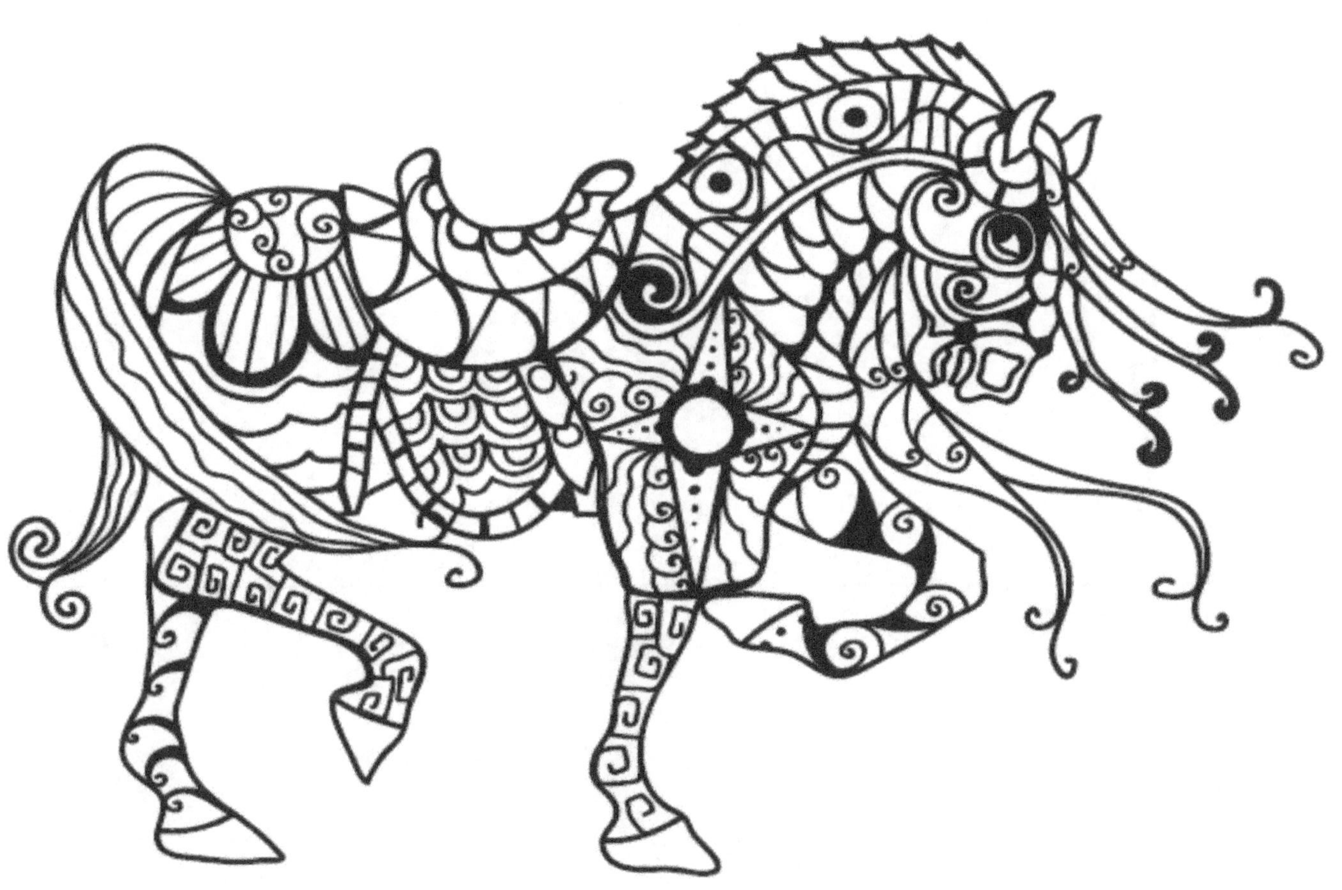

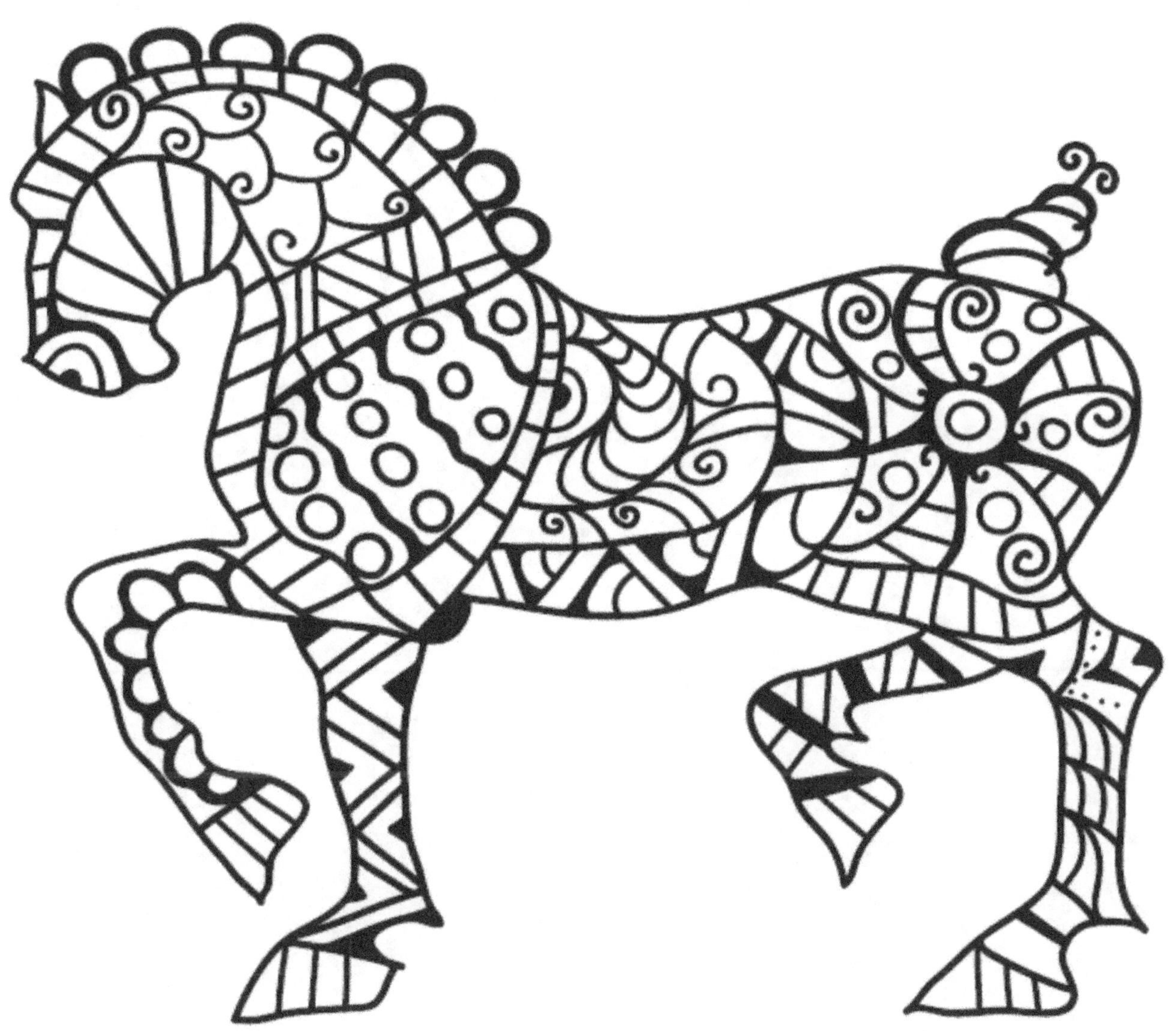

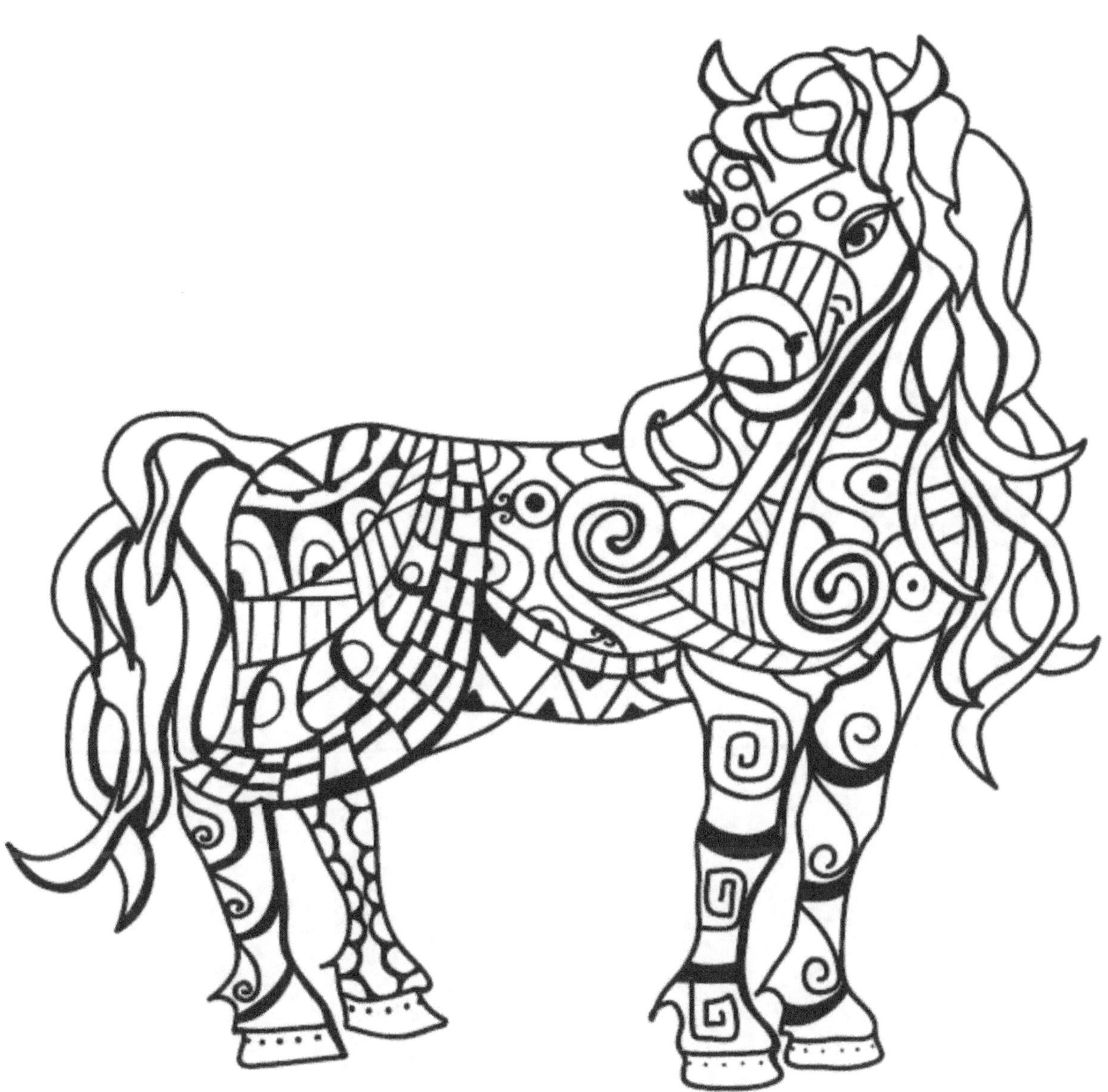

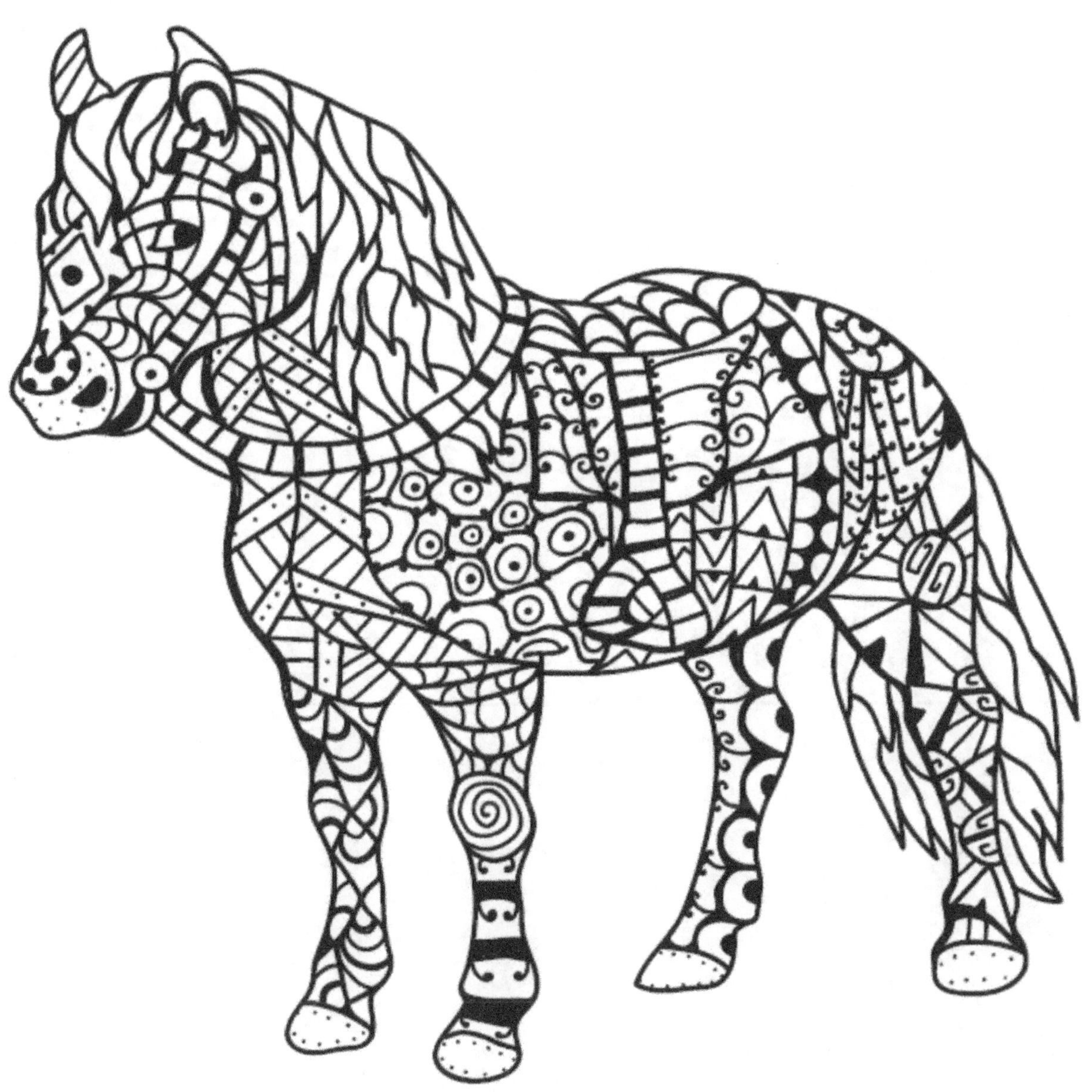

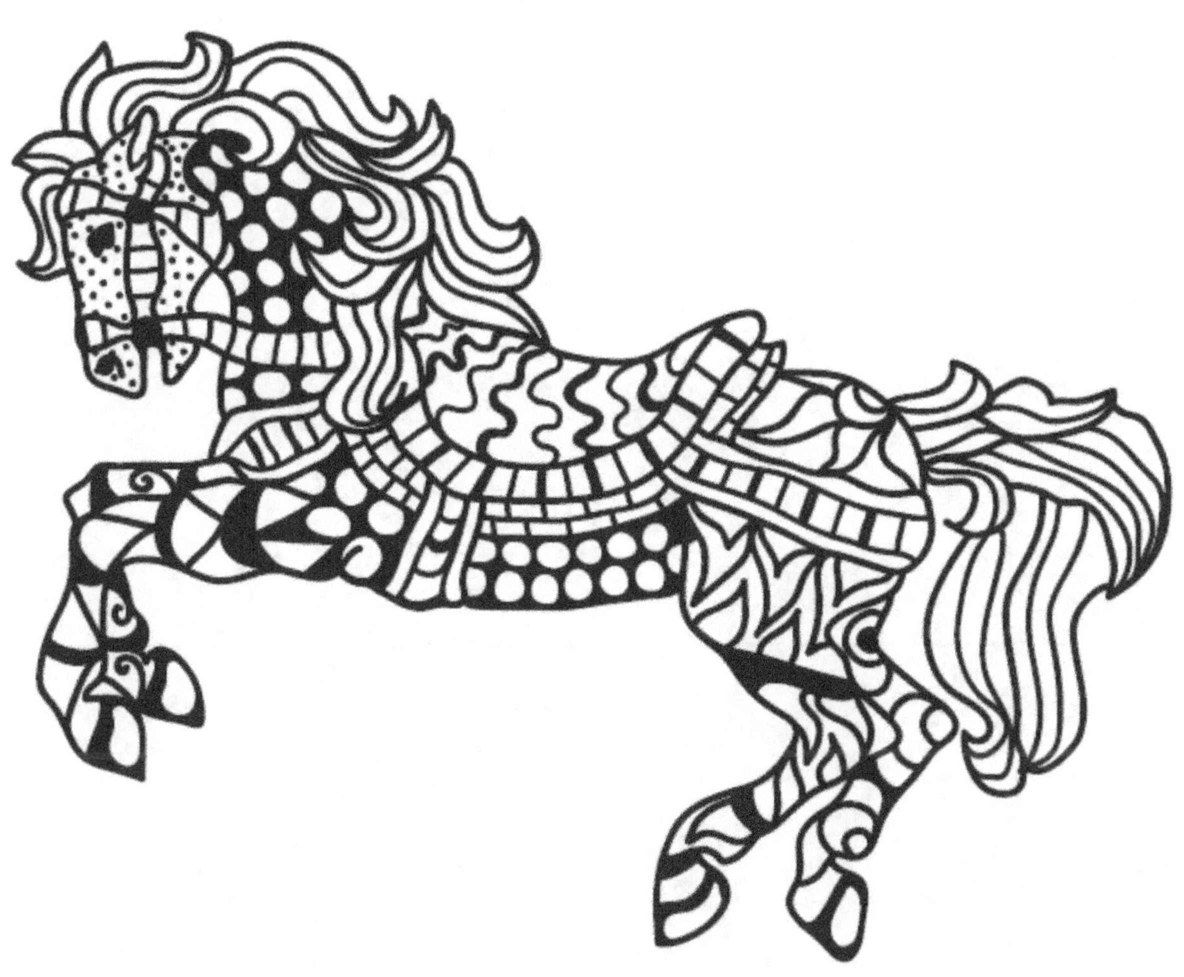

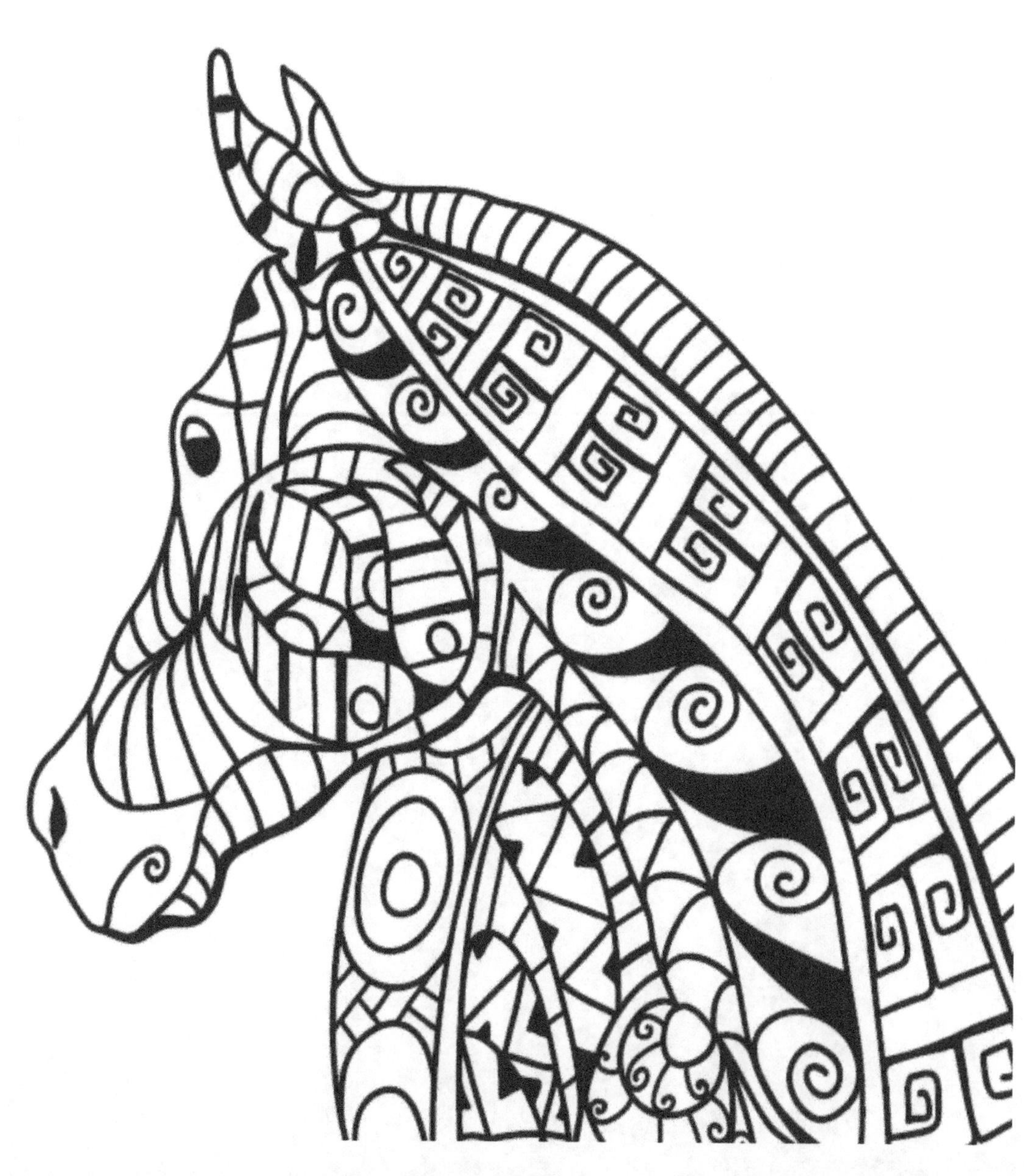

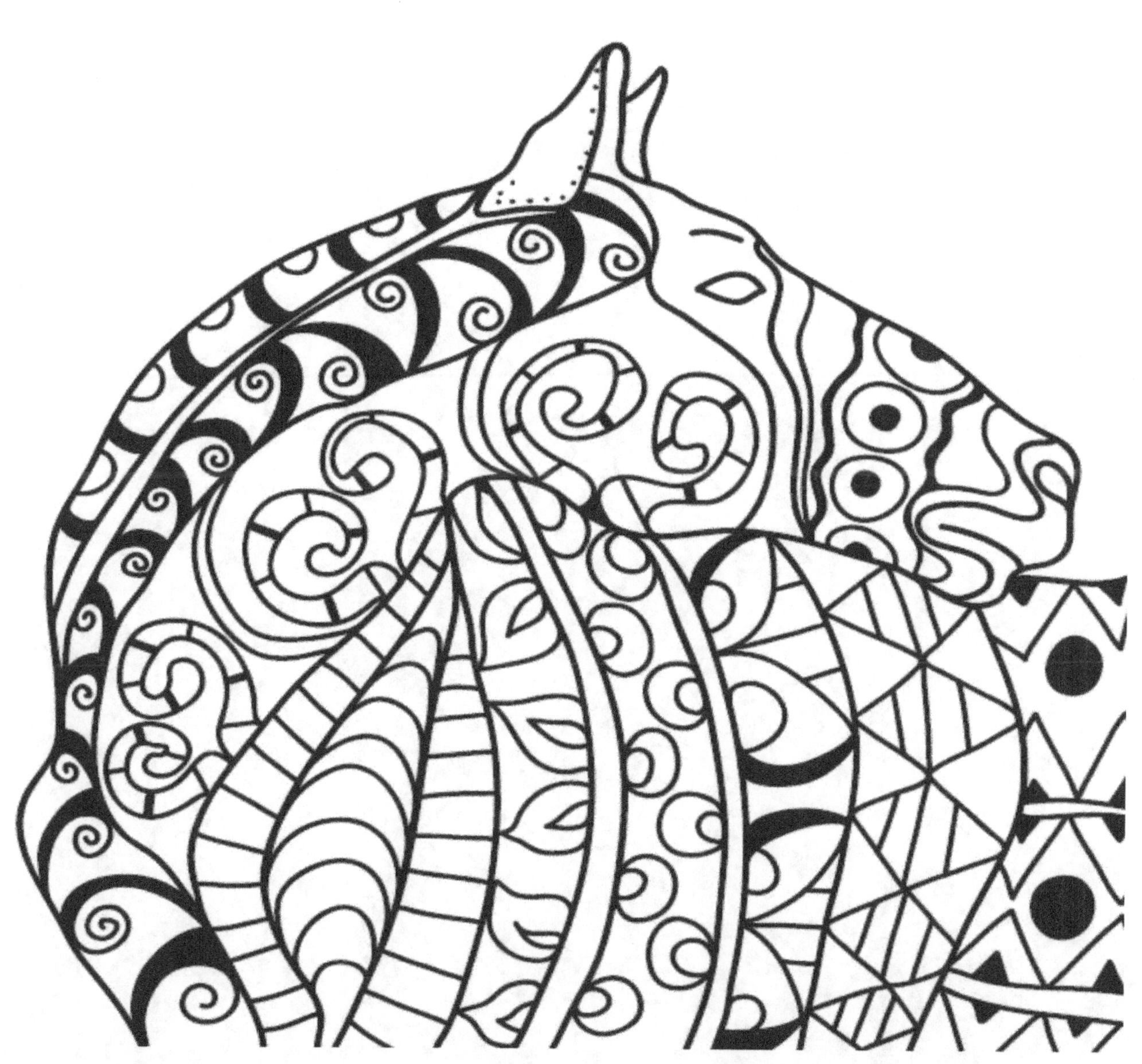

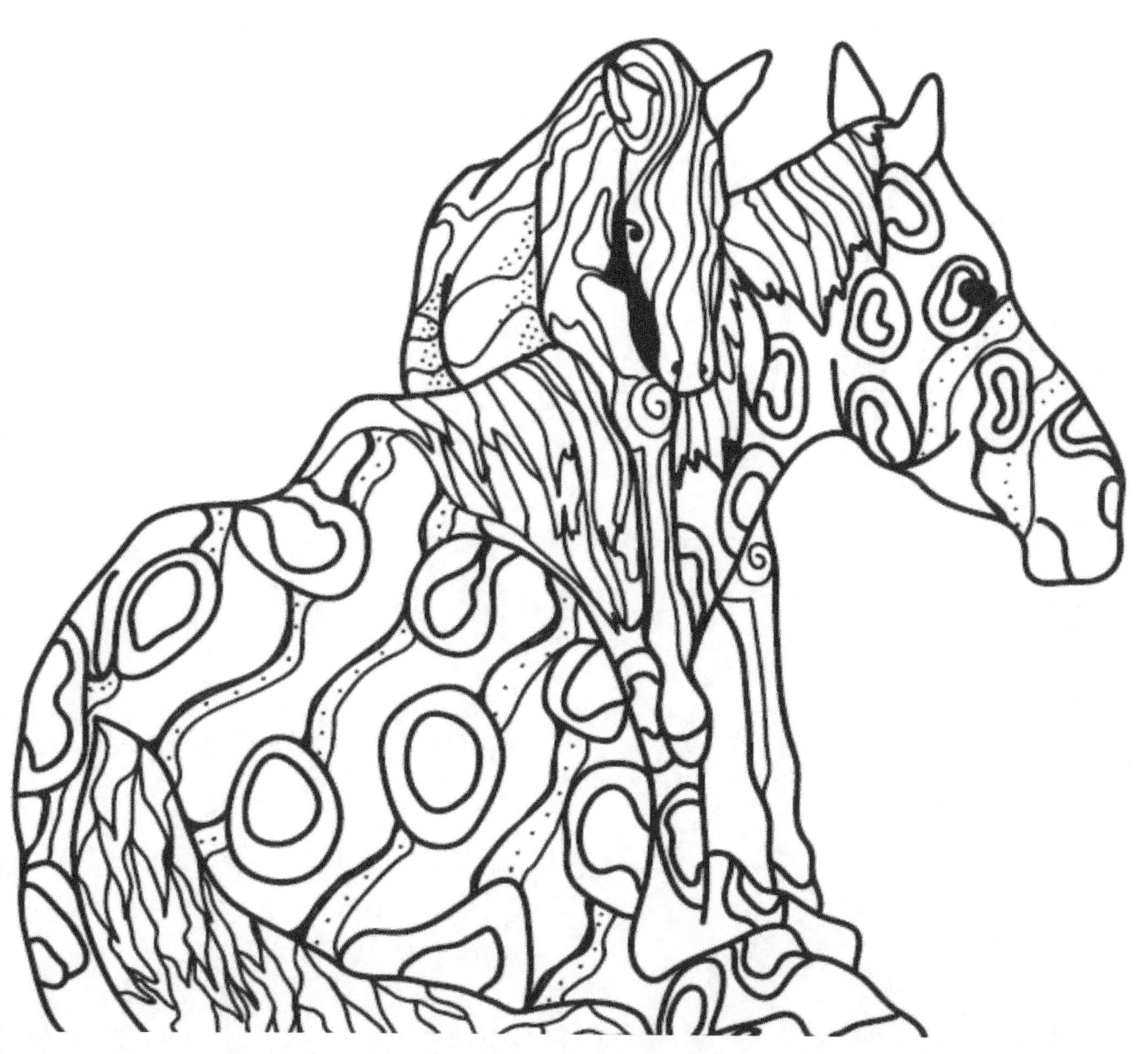

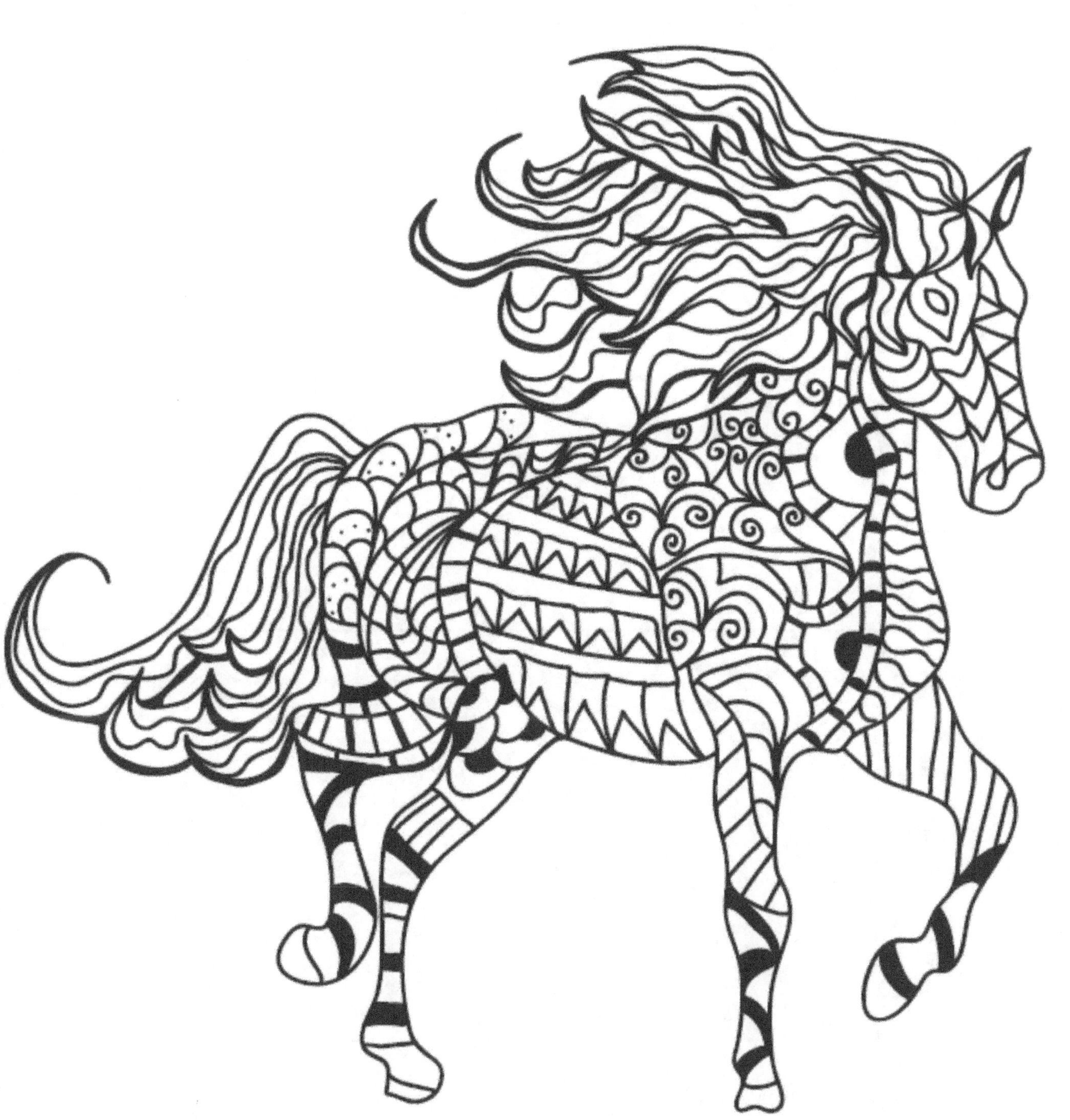

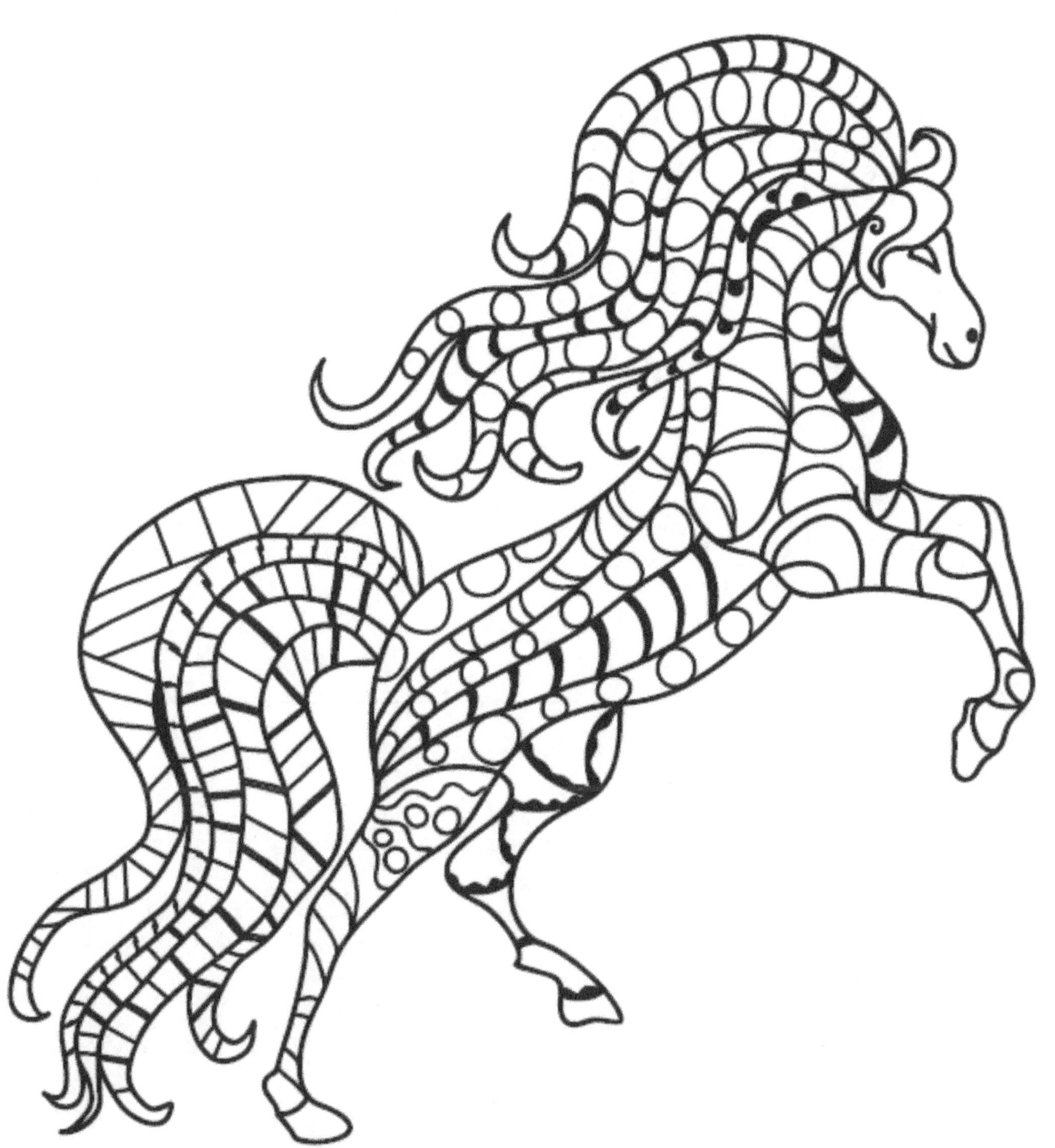

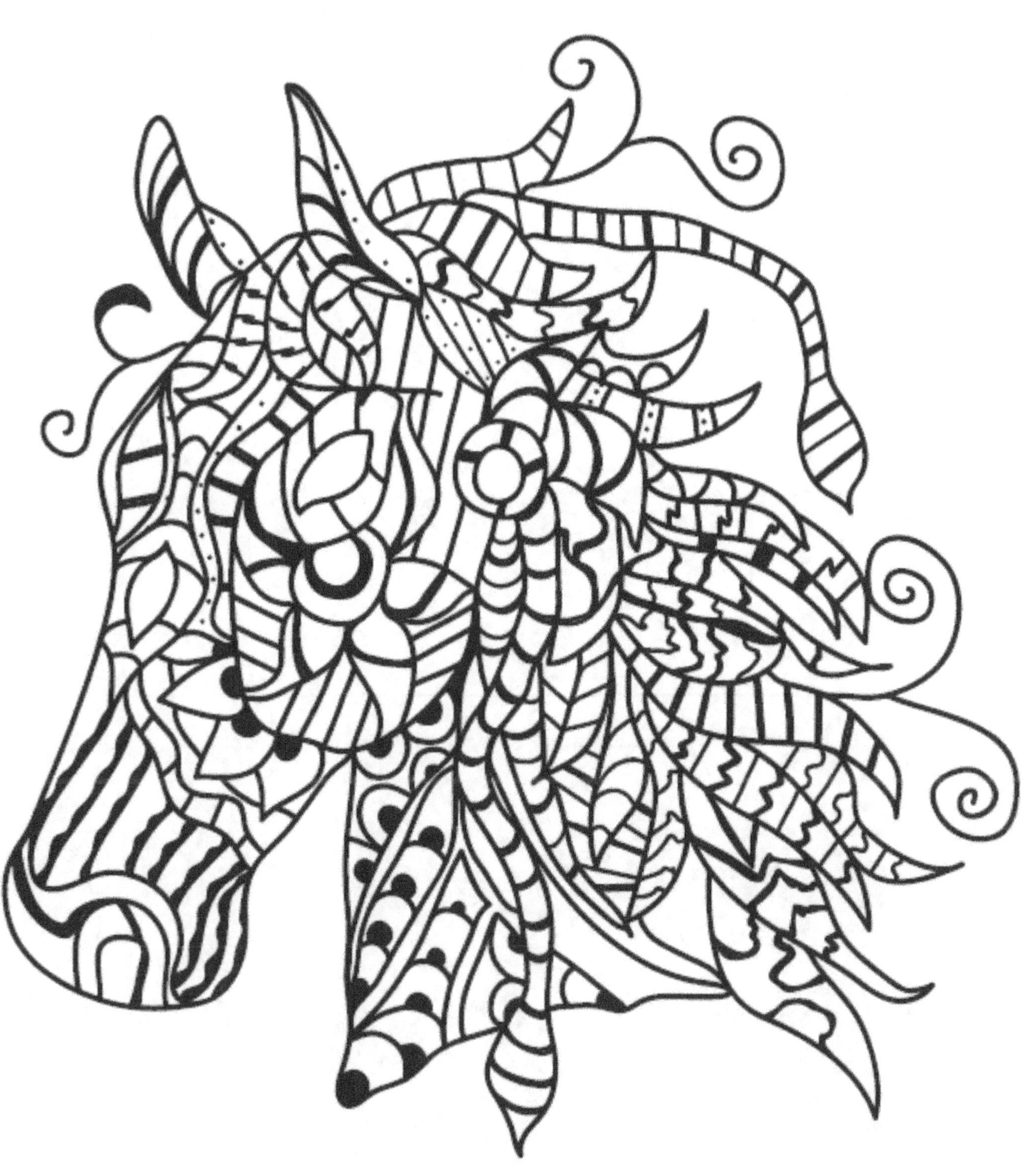

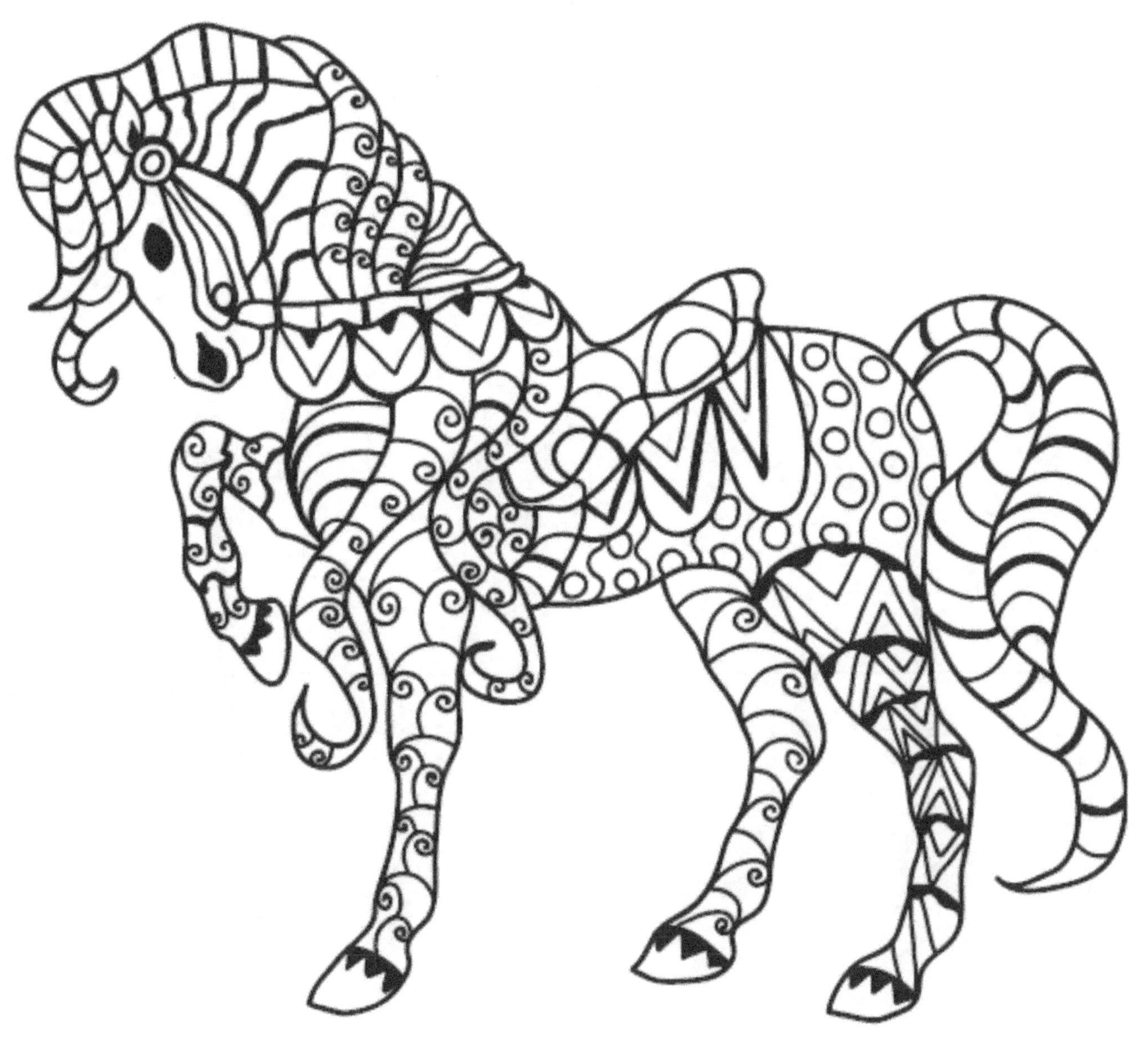

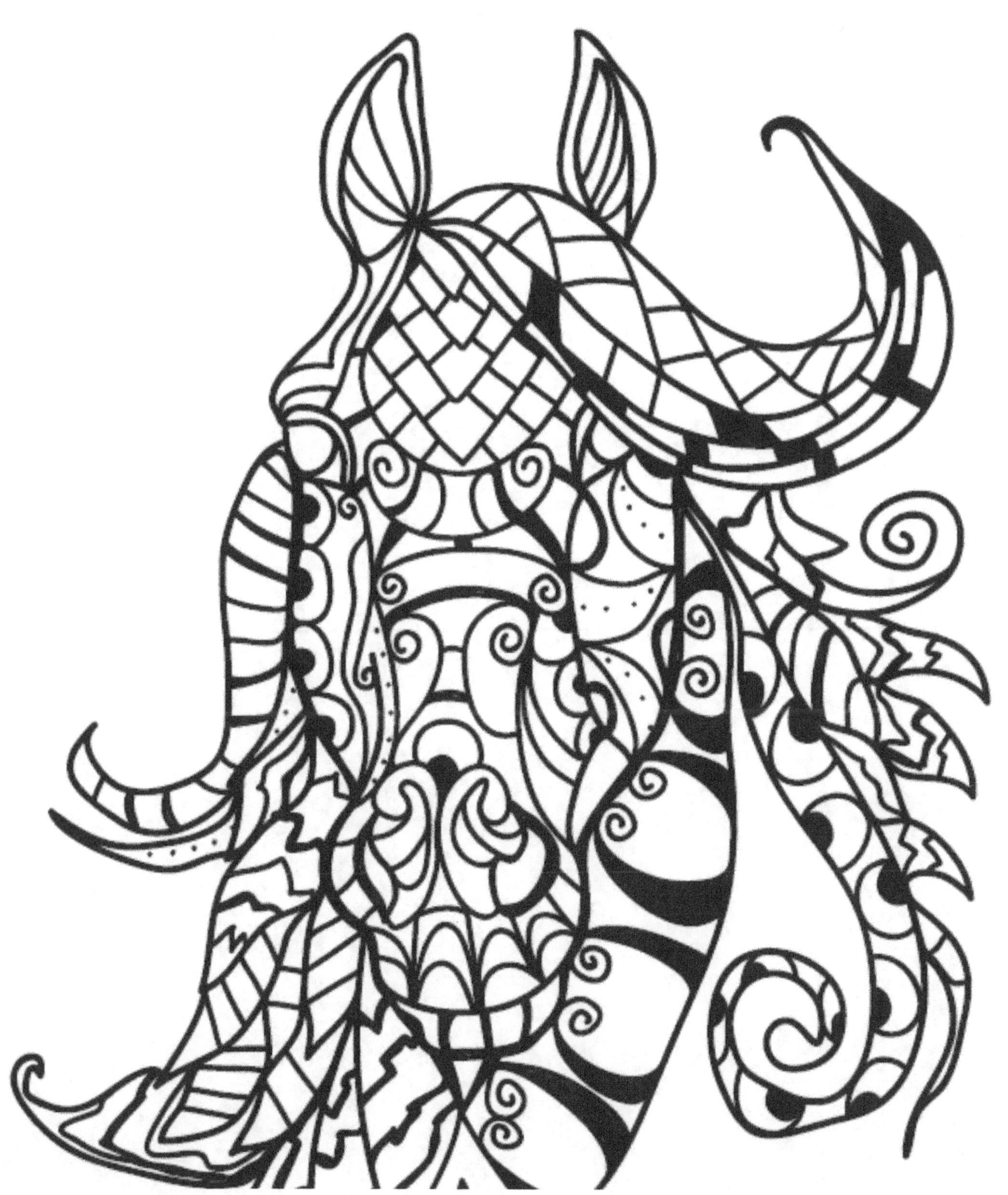

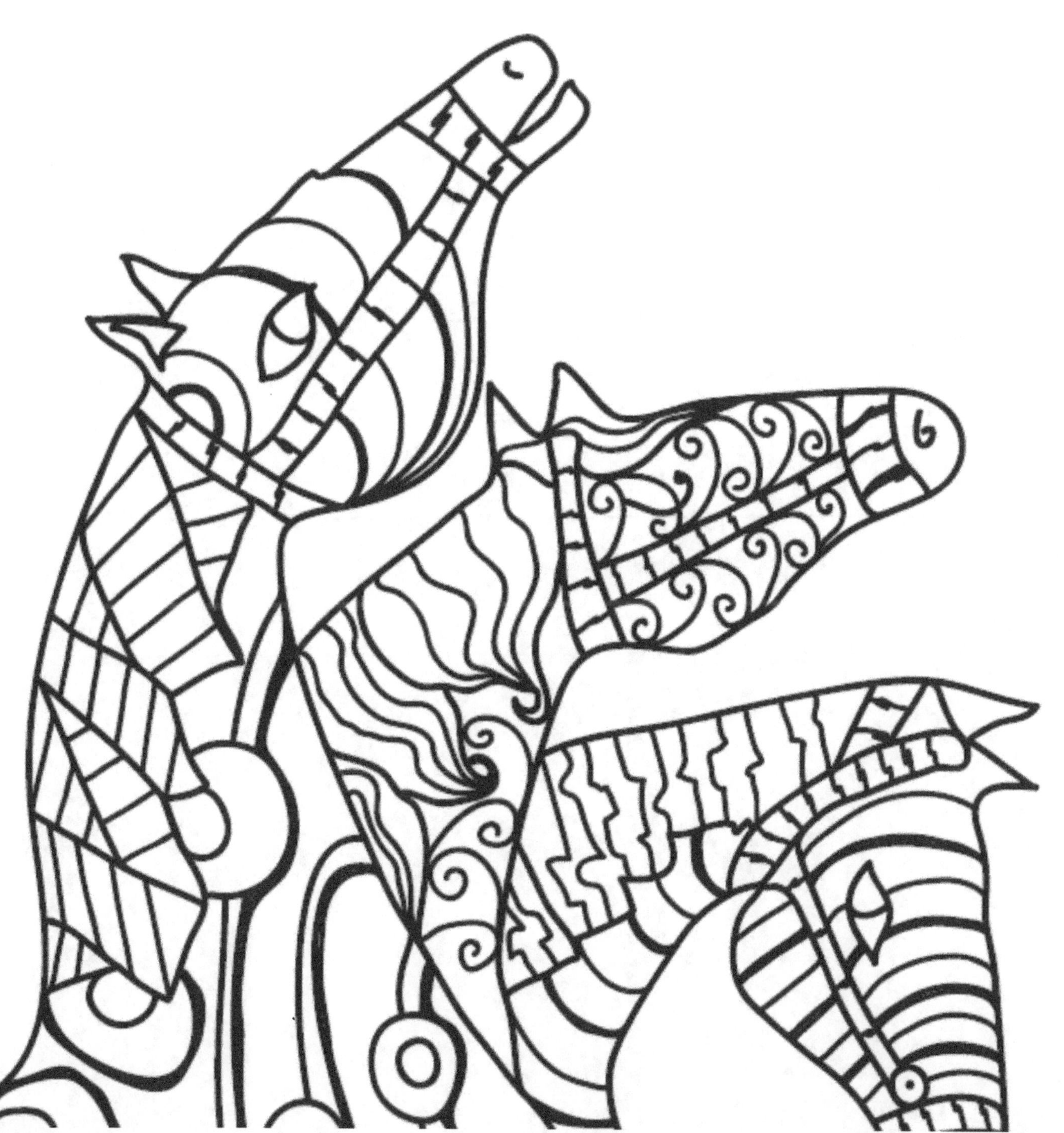

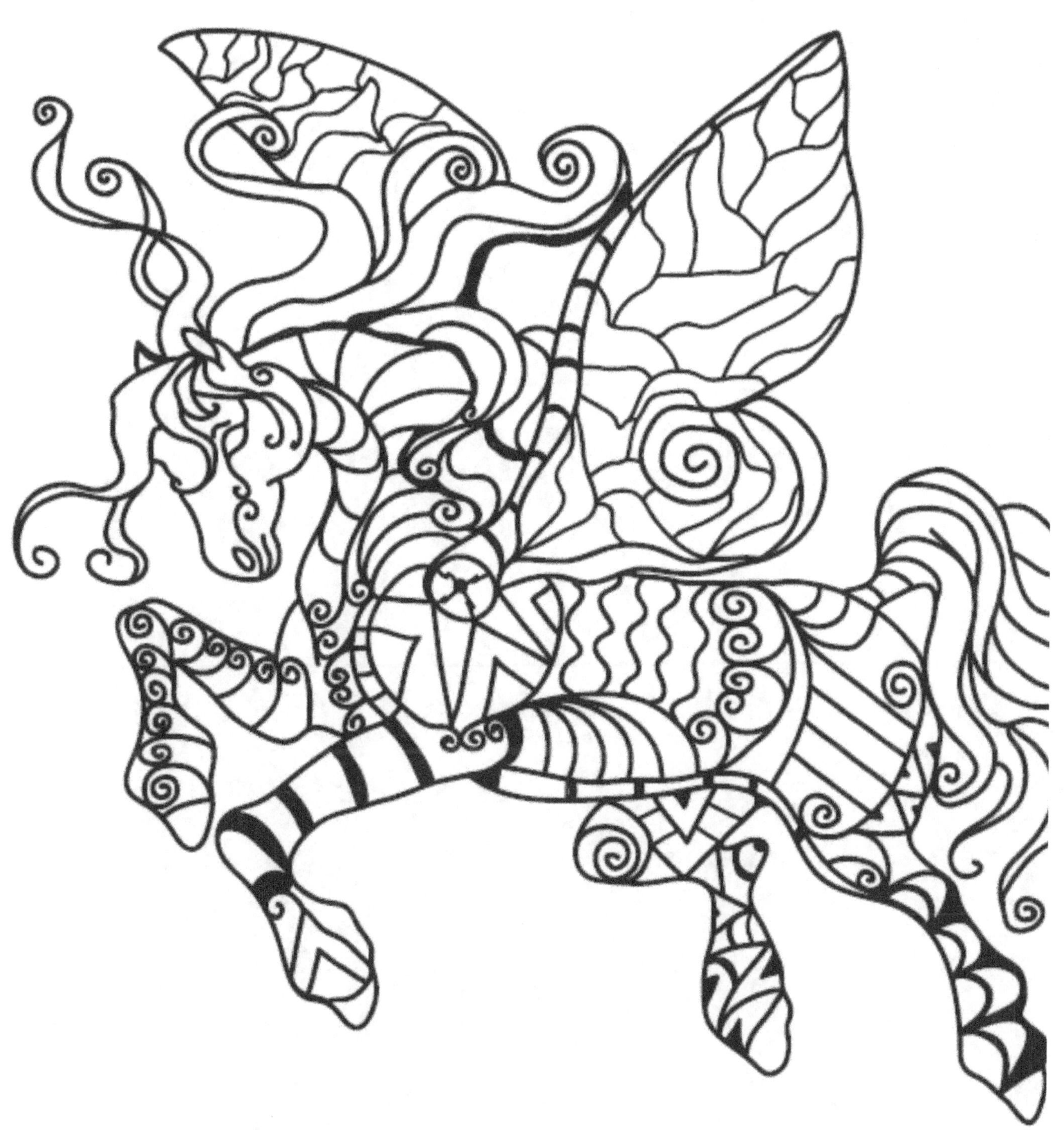

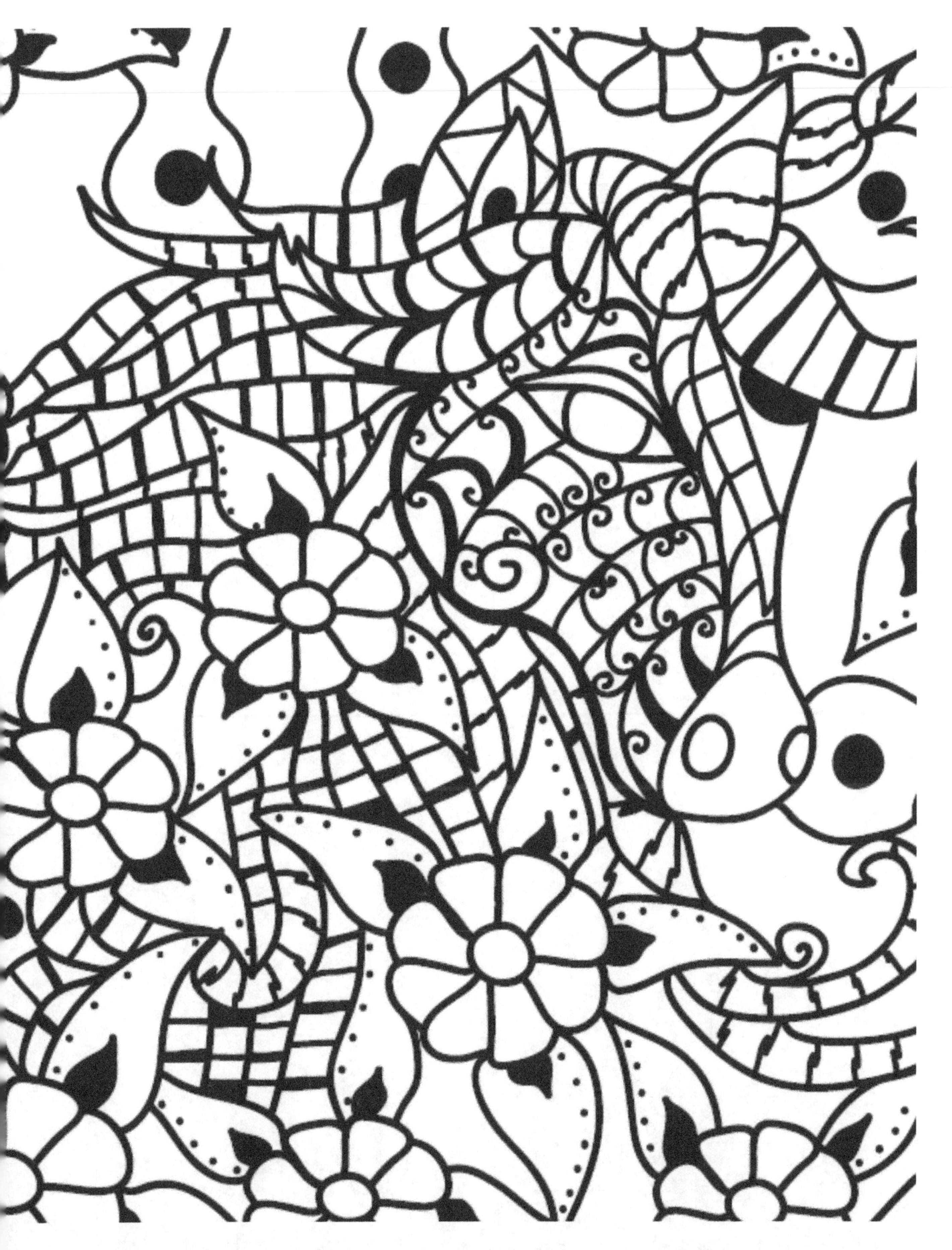

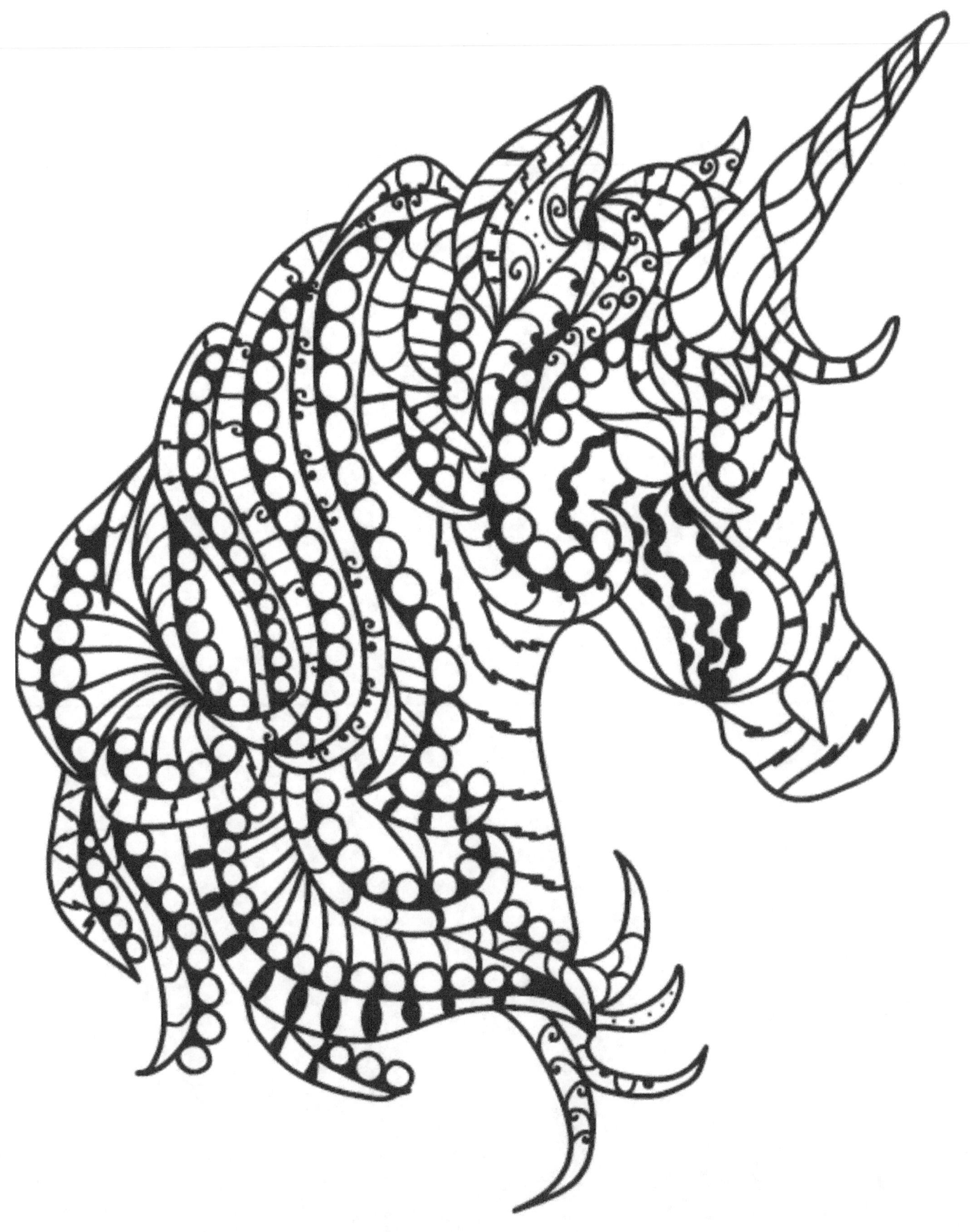

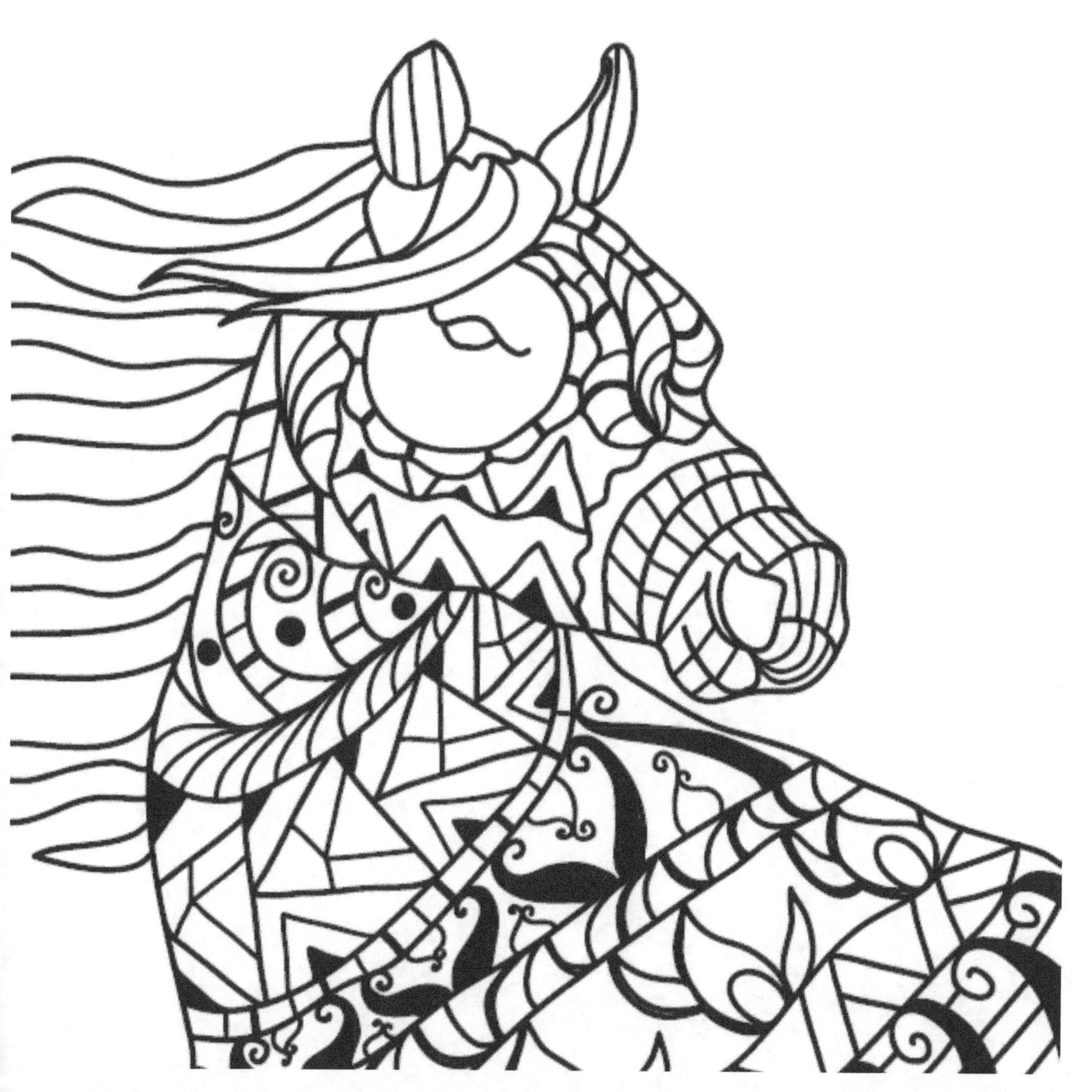

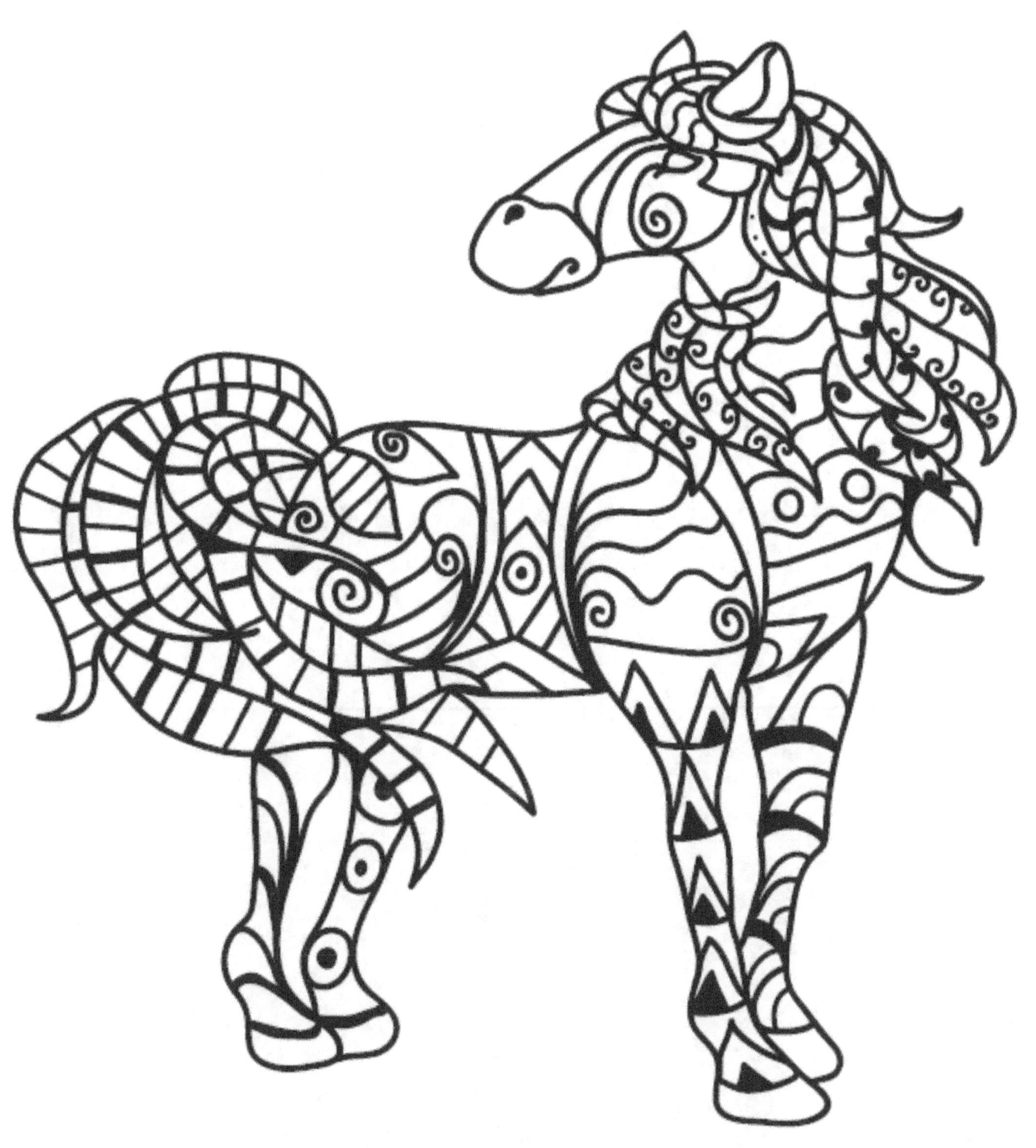

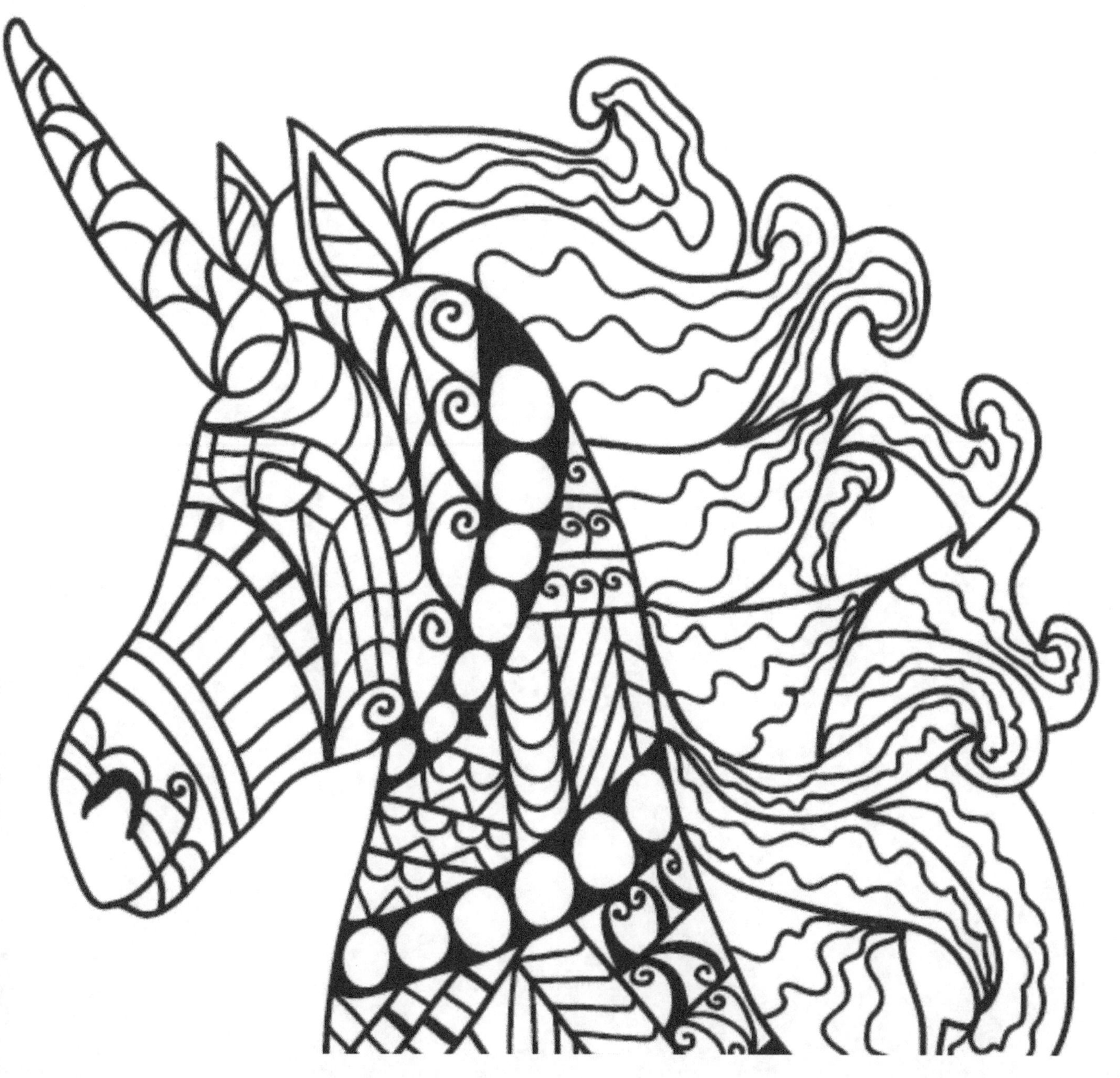

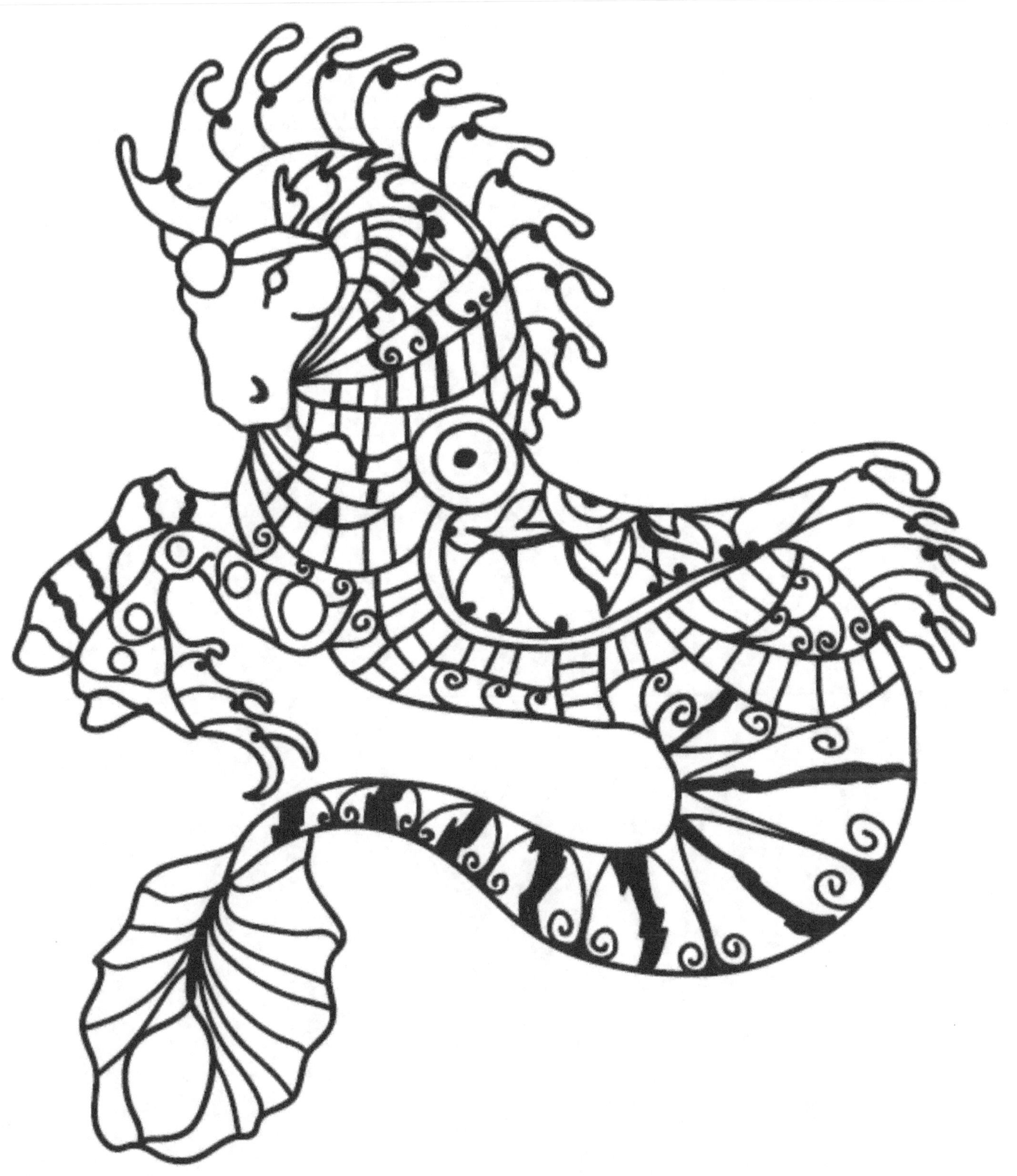

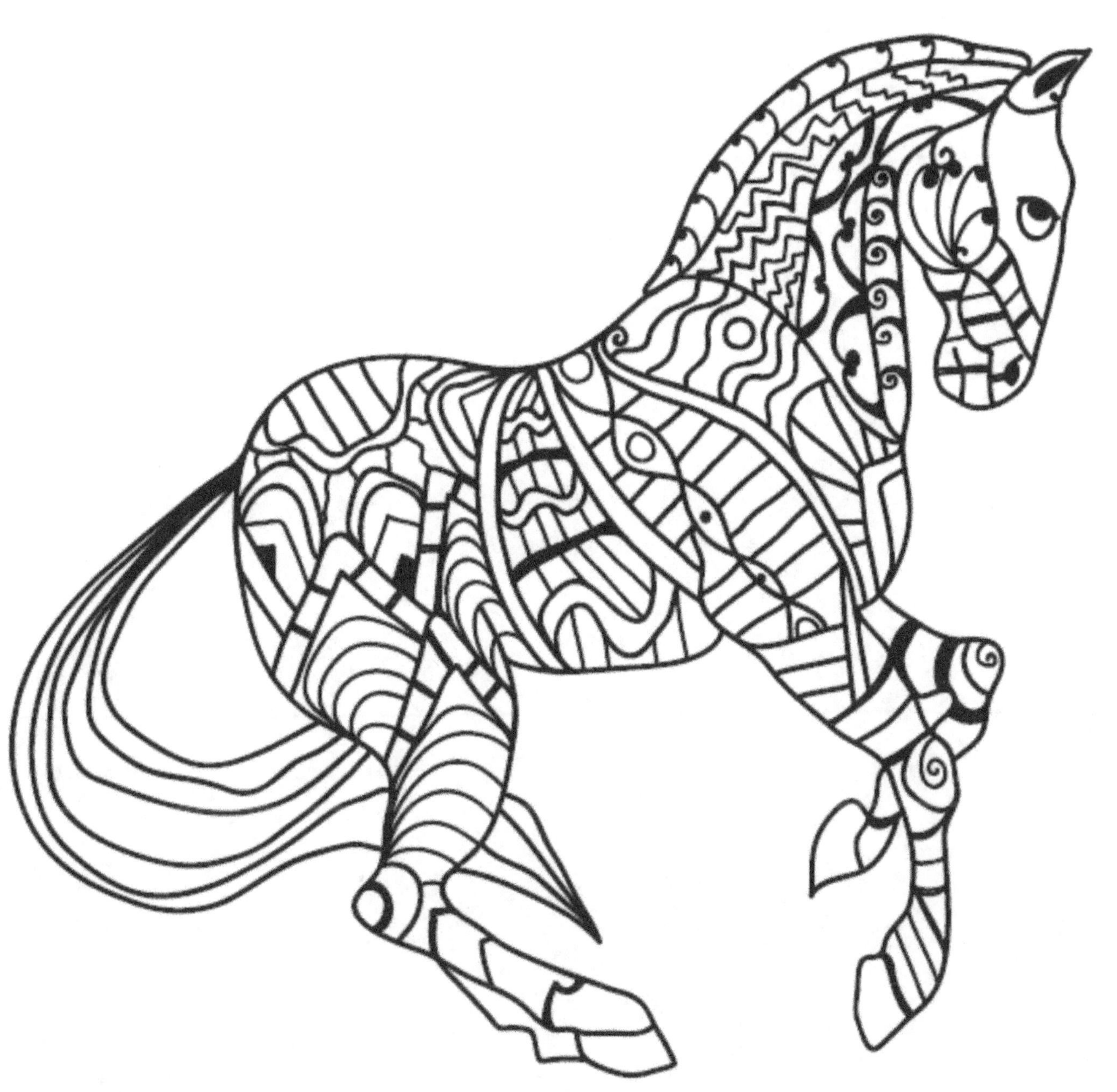

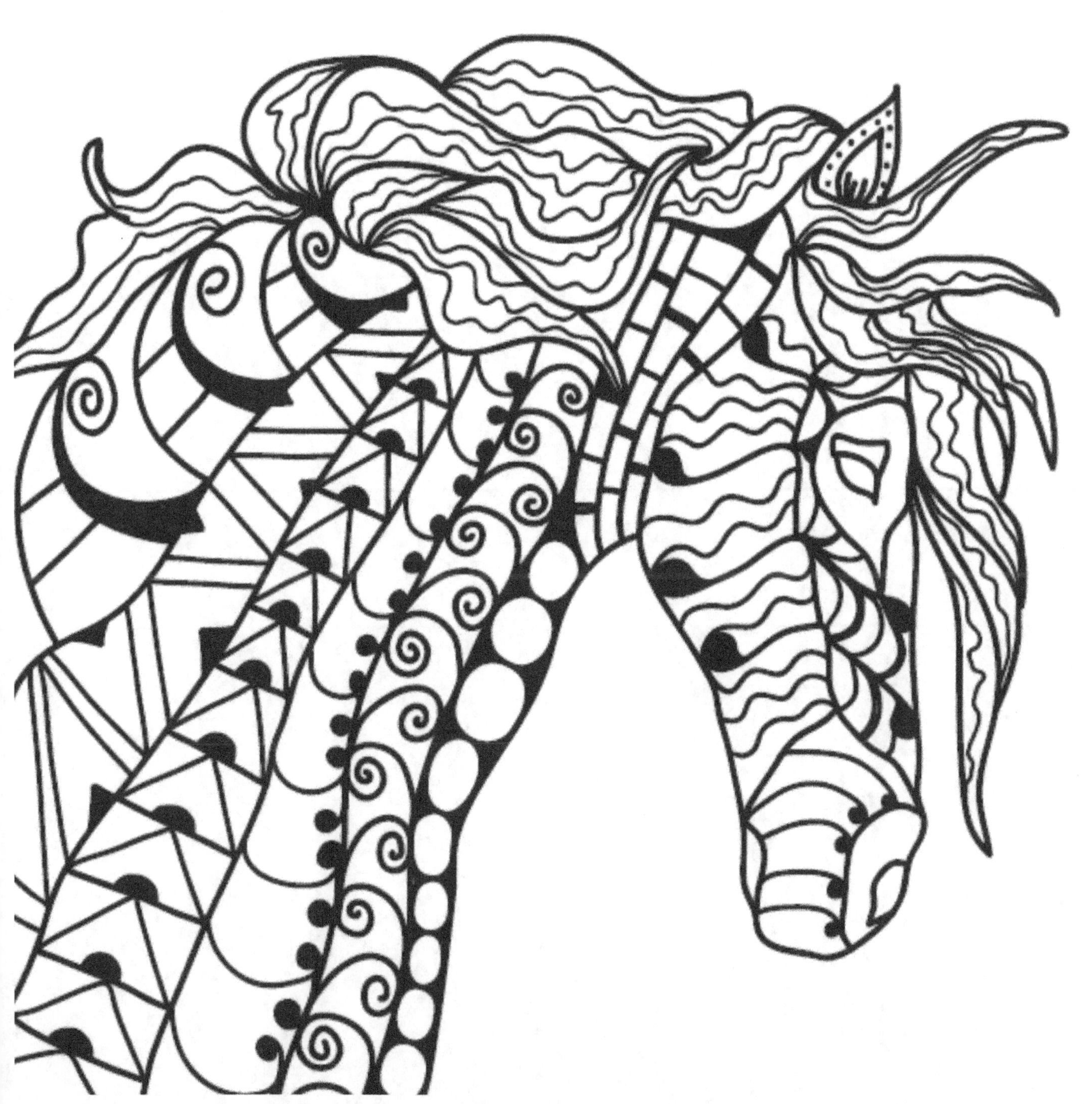

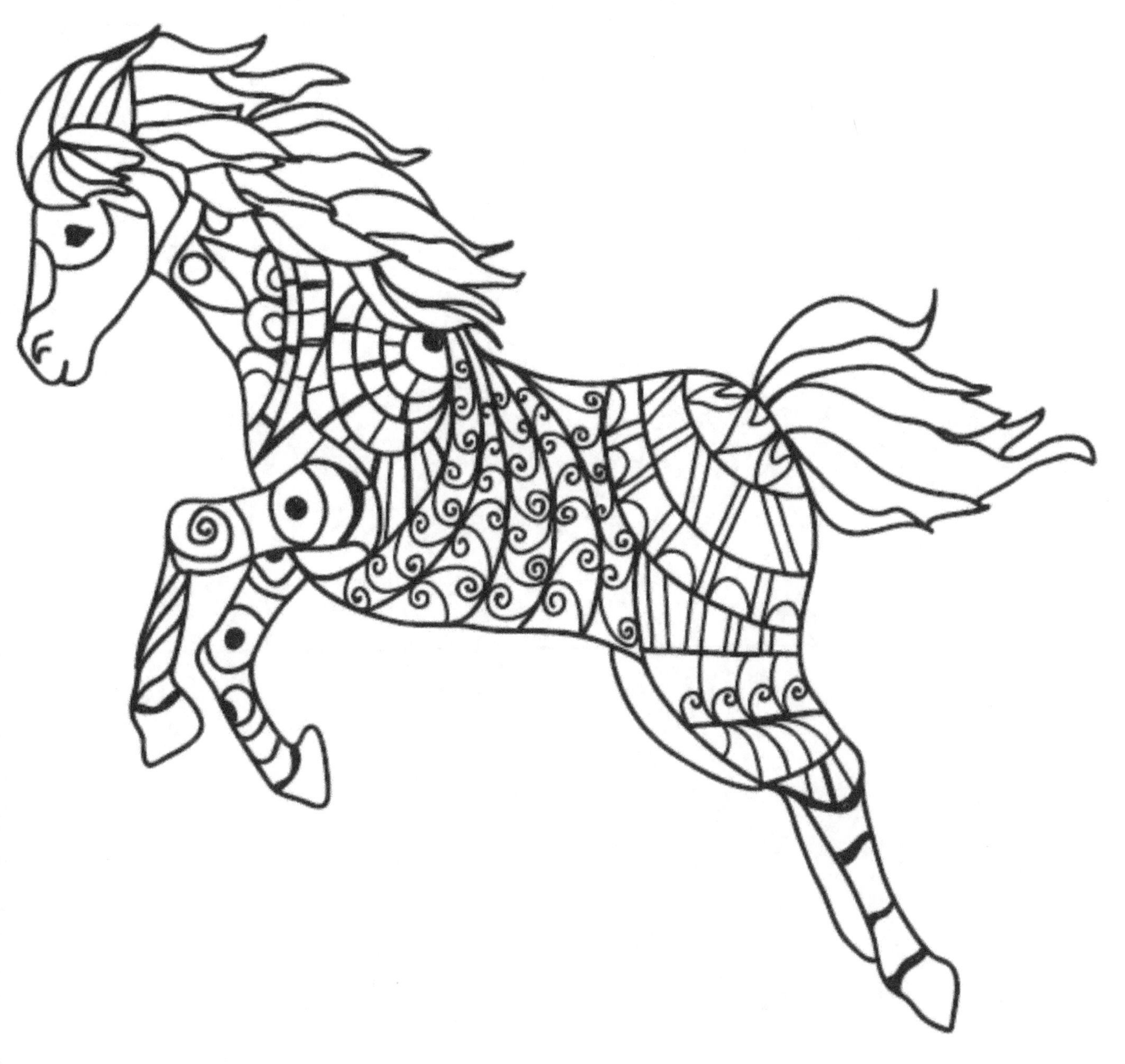

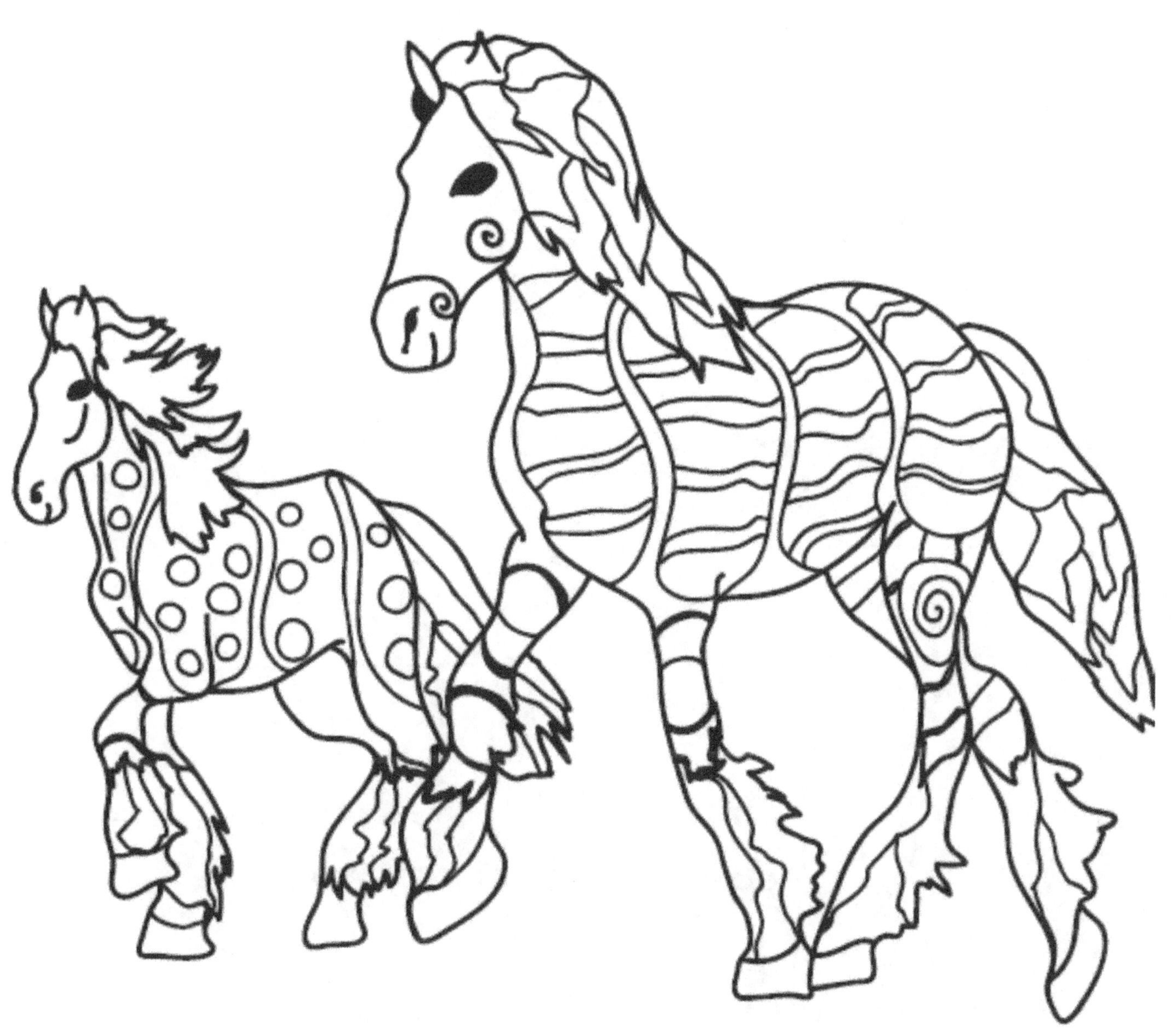

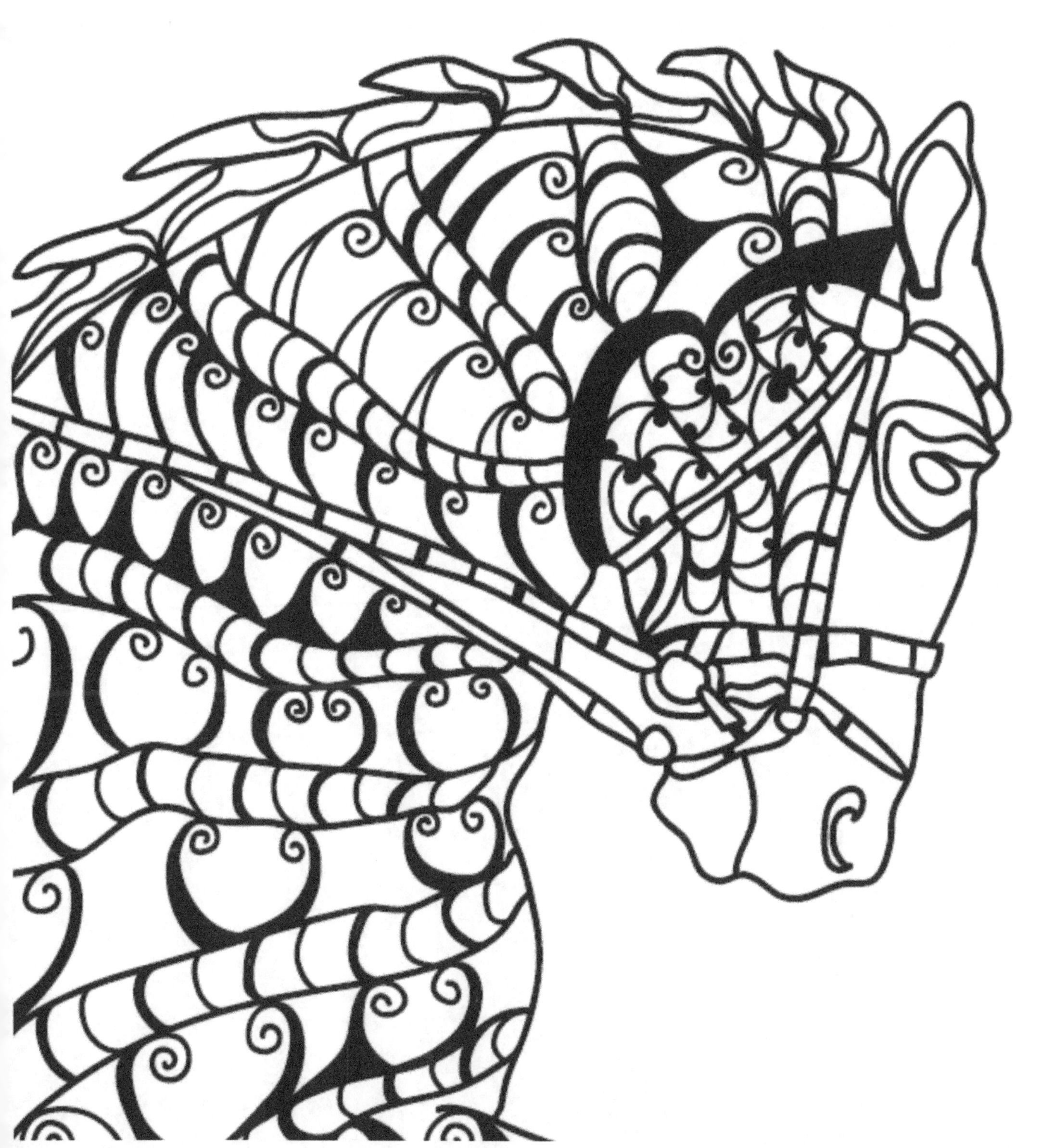

Horse Coloring Pages

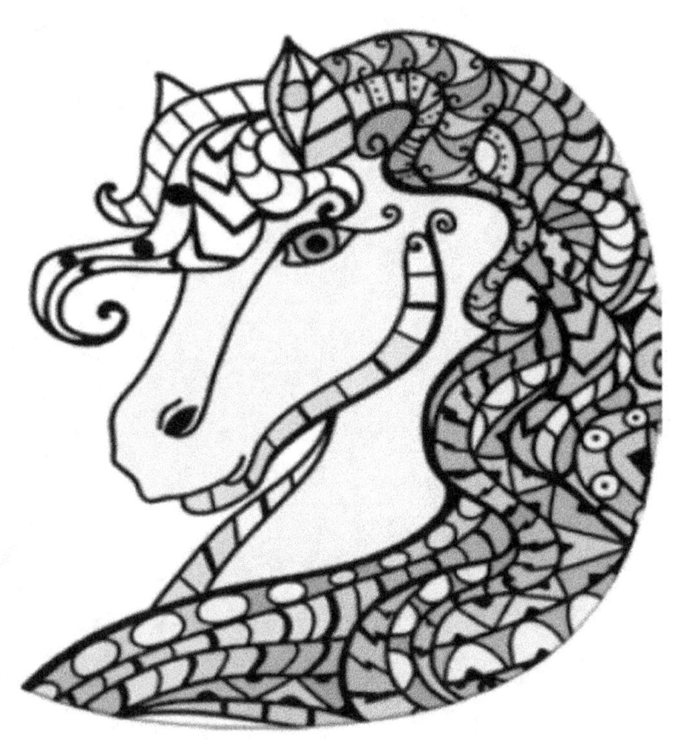

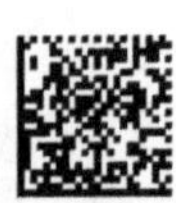

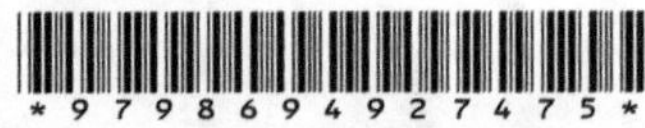
9 798869 492747 5